Votewise 2015

Votewise 2015

Making a difference at the ballot box and beyond

Guy Brandon

First published in Great Britain in 2014

Society for Promoting Christian Knowledge
36 Causton Street
London SW1P 4ST
www.spckpublishing.co.uk

British Library Cataloguing-in-Publication Data
A catalogue record for this book is available from the British Library

ISBN 978-0-281-07178-4
eBook ISBN 978-0-281-07179-1

Typeset by Caroline Waldron, Wirral, Cheshire
Manufacture managed by Jellyfish
First printed in Great Britain by CPI Group
Subsequently digitally printed in Great Britain

eBook by Graphicraft Limited, Hong Kong

Produced on paper from sustainable forests

Contents

1

Engaging with politics

Introduction: the new political landscape

'The past is a foreign country: they do things differently there.'
L. P. Hartley's often repeated words have particular resonance for
the 2015 General Election. Over the past five years, the UK's
political landscape has changed out of all recognition. For decades the country effectively operated under a two-party system,
with tribal blocs of voters remaining fiercely loyal to the Conservative or Labour parties. As the first edition of *Votewise* noted:

> It used to be so easy. You were either for individualism,
> small government and the free market or for collectivism,
> big government and nationalization. The answer to the
> UK's problems was to reduce government interference and
> allow families and businesses to run their own affairs, or to
> redistribute wealth from the affluent to the needy and let
> the state run industry. You were motivated by choice and
> freedom or by fairness and equality.[1]

For a long time the limited ground between these two positions
was sparsely populated, and despite the existence of other parties – particularly the rise of the Liberal Democrats – none had
ever interfered with a working majority for either the Conservatives or Labour to any significant degree. Even when the
lines became more and more blurred, a majority for one or
other was practically a foregone conclusion. That was just how
we did government.

Politicians have made a refrain of promising change, but in
2010 it came from an unlikely source: voters. Unlikely, because
voters had become increasingly apathetic over the course of the

previous government. In the 1990s, sleaze and corruption led to disillusionment with all politicians – not just John Major's government – and the shift away from traditional political boundaries meant that voters found it harder to distinguish the parties from one another. Even when Tony Blair secured his landslide victory in 1997, he did so on the lowest turnout since 1935. Political journalist Andrew Rawnsley comments:

> Fewer than one in three of the potential electorate had put a cross by the name of a Labour candidate. As the defeated Major would bitterly remark, Blair had secured his obese parliamentary majority of 179 with half a million fewer votes in ballot boxes than had five years earlier given Major an anorexic majority of twenty-one.[2]

Labour won with the backing of 43.2 per cent of those who did turn out to vote. In the 1950s it had *lost* elections with a greater proportion of voters' support.

The trend continued in 2001, with turnout falling below 60 per cent for the first time since 1918. It was only marginally higher in 2005. Fed up with a government that seemed remote from their everyday concerns and with politicians of all hues dogged by corruption and scandal, the public expressed its anger by staying at home. Voters wanted something different and – understandably – if they couldn't find it then they weren't going to bother making the trip to the polling station at all.

Something different

The political landscape changed dramatically in 2010. Dismay at the effects of the Global Financial Crisis and fury over the parliamentary expenses scandal had shocked voters into realizing that 'business as usual' was not an option. Neither main party looked like a good deal for the country, and the polls were uncomfortably close. For a while, voters thought they had found their 'something different' in the TV debates that took place for the first time in British politics. Nick Clegg, the leader of the Liberal Democrats, used the opportunity to cast his party as the untainted outsider to Westminster and the answer to the dilemma of two tired and all-too-similar alternatives. 'The more they attack each other, the more they sound the same,' he told his captivated audience. But the 'Cleggmania' bounce his party received in public support – some polls showed the Lib Dems briefly pushing Labour into third place – failed to translate into seats at the election. The public returned no single party to power, circumstances that brought about the country's first full coalition government since the Second World War. The Liberal Democrats entered government not because the public liked them more than the other two parties, but because they liked neither Conservatives nor Labour enough to elect a majority.

Coalition government did not prove a popular solution. In many countries it is the norm, but the UK is not used to it: before 2010 the last full coalition was in 1945. Most voters want one party in charge. In the early days the Lib Dems bore the brunt of voters' displeasure, with support for the party slumping into single figures by the end of the year. Once seen as the party who would hold the Conservatives to account, the Lib Dems left some of their supporters feeling betrayed by a series of compromises forced on the party by the tough realities of governing in a coalition: U-turns on university tuition fees and the 'mansion tax' particularly disappointed some who had voted them into power.

The future's purple?

Two years out from the 2015 election, a bright new alternative presented itself to the electorate. The UK Independence Party surged into the popular consciousness around the 2013 local elections, fuelled by anti-Europe sentiment and their fresh critique of the political establishment. Being in government had robbed the Lib Dems of their position as untarnished outsiders to Westminster, and they joined the two tainted brands of Labour, blamed for bringing about the financial crisis, and the Conservatives, blamed for not fixing the problem more quickly and fairly.

Now, the UK had a new party of protest. From struggling as a fringe party for many years – once memorably dismissed as 'fruitcakes, loonies and closet racists' by David Cameron – UKIP suddenly became a major player. In the popular vote, at least, polls showed they would easily overtake the Lib Dems as the third largest party. However, the first past the post system heavily disadvantages parties like UKIP, which have broad but evenly spread support across the country. The Green Party won its first ever seat in 2010 with far lower national backing thanks to strong local support in Brighton; UKIP has no such 'heartlands' and will need to win at least 20 per cent of the popular vote in order to gain many seats in the General Election. What is far more likely is that voters switching to UKIP will decrease the number of Conservative MPs, despite the ground the latter gain thanks to a recovering economy.

No one wins

Coalition politics is not a popular solution, but it is a possible one. A week is a long time in politics, as Harold Wilson said, and everything can and does change at the last minute. And, of course, the polls can be wrong – sometimes spectacularly so, as in 1992, when polls pointing to a narrow Labour victory belied a Conservative majority on the day. But for a number of reasons, a second coalition government is still a real possibility. The rise of UKIP as a fourth party creates greater fragmentation at the expense of all the other parties, though especially the Conservatives. A small swing in support for UKIP could hand the election to one of the major parties, or to neither.

And that raises the possibility of no one getting what they want. In the run-up to the election the different parties will each articulate their vision for the United Kingdom in the knowledge that they may well have to compromise if they are to govern at all – in fact, even before the election they may be working to identify promises they can leave behind if a coalition partner demands it. Add an extensive list of scandals and it's no wonder that public attitudes towards politics and politicians have been shaken. Political party membership and voter turnout have collapsed and overall confidence is at an all-time low. If turnout follows the recent trend for General Elections, it could be lower than at any time in the last century.[3]

Christian democracy

Where does the Christian faith fit into this picture? The UK is very different from many other democracies around the world in that its culture generally does not explicitly combine its politics with religion. None of the major political parties has a strong Christian bias or appeal – unlike in America, where faith and politics go hand in hand and the Republicans enjoy significant support from evangelical Christians. And there are no success-ful overtly Christian parties – unlike on the Continent, where many Christian democratic parties exist and have enough popu-lar support to participate in government. The Conservatives used to provide a natural home for socially conservative Christians, but have drifted from this position in recent years. Labour's roots as the party of fairness and social justice have appealed to many Christians, and Tony Blair's own faith might have provided a natural focus for believers had not such pains been taken to keep it separate from his public life. Alastair Campbell famously intervened to stop Blair talking about his faith, and 'We don't do God'[4] became (somewhat unfairly) the take-home message about the Labour Party's approach to Christianity. There are outspoken Christians within the Liberal Democrats, as there are within the Conservatives and Labour, but Nick Clegg's avowed atheism sets the tone for the party. UKIP's collection of policies has not resonated fully enough with Christians to capture their protest vote successfully.

And yet faith is undeniably woven throughout politics in the UK. Some of our most dearly held political ideas – including our identity as a nation, the importance of due process of law, the idea of politics as service, human equality, even democracy itself – have been fundamentally shaped by the Bible.[5] Sittings in both the House of Commons and the House of Lords still begin with Christian prayers, as they have done for around 450 years.

Neither is faith just an ancient rubber stamp on the day's political activities. Some of the biggest and freshest political developments of recent times have been informed by Christian ideas. Politicians on both left and right have openly drawn on Christian thinking in their search for answers to the economic crisis. Catholic Social Teaching underpinned the Big Society initiative, as well as informing the Red Tory and Blue Labour movements.[6] From different sides of the political spectrum, both Red Tory and Blue Labour diagnose the same problem: that families, communities and the many different groups that make up civil society have found themselves increasingly squeezed between the state and the market. As these two giants grow, people become more reliant on them – burdened by debt and dependent on welfare – to the detriment of the networks of support they once enjoyed. Red Tory and Blue Labour both emphasize the need for a more moral form of capitalism and a limit to state activity, though they differ on how to achieve this.

So, both historically and in the present, the Christian faith can provide foundations for and influence upon the political narrative. And yet we remain decidedly ambivalent about the relationship between faith and politics. During the prayers that are spoken before sittings in the Houses of Parliament, members of the public are banned from entering the public galleries and those present turn to face the wall behind them: an apt metaphor for the role many politicians allow faith in public life.[7]

Principles, not policy

Whereas the teachings of the New Testament are largely concerned with the faith and conduct of Christians living in a pagan environment, the Old Testament is concerned with how God's people organized themselves and behaved as a nation. Although, as Christians, we always read the Old Testament in the light of Jesus' coming, it is to OT Law that we first look when seeking biblical insights into questions of how to run the country.

Old Testament Israel was a theocracy: the only law was passed down to the people from God through Moses. We now live in a democracy, and our laws are created by elected politicians who may or may not share our faith. Applying laws directly from the Bible to modern life would be unpopular (because a large proportion of the electorate don't share those Judaeo-Christian convictions), unworkable (owing to the gulf between second-millennium BC Israel and the twenty-first-century UK), and decidedly unwise. We cannot (and would not want to) expect a secular government to enforce policies lifted straight from a biblical legal framework. With those problems in mind, how can our Christian faith meaningfully inform our political engagement?

Many of the specific *policies* found in the Bible would seem bizarre or distasteful to modern ears: the death penalty for adulterers, the seven-year cancellation of debt and compulsory rest from work on the Sabbath being just three examples. But the *principles* that lie behind these laws – such as the importance of family stability, economic sustainability and protection for low-income and marginalized workers – are a different matter. The application of those principles in the Bible was shaped by the Israelites' historical circumstances, their status as God's chosen people and the cultural constraints of the time. But the principles themselves are unchanging, and have just as much relevance today as they did then. So, we are on firmer ground with principles.

The reality is that politics always works with principles, even if those principles are obscure. Behind every policy that wins the headlines there are assumptions about what is good and what is bad. These are the values that a party reveals through its policies, whether or not they are explicitly aligned with its stated message. Critics often claim that Christian ideals have no place in modern politics. But *no* political principle or policy can be morally neutral. There is always some assumption about what is right and wrong. The belief that either the state or the market is best able to serve the interests of citizens forms the traditional dividing line between left and right, for example. Christian values may have just as much place in the political sphere as those of any other ideology. The challenge for Christians in politics is to set Christian values favourably alongside other ideologies in a way that allows the public to assess their merits.

The policies that the different parties offer in their election manifestos will reflect their principles – principles that may be more or less closely aligned with those found in the Bible. The aim of *Votewise 2015* is to give readers a strong and coherent biblical framework for assessing the principles, policies and promises that each party makes in its bid to govern the country. It does not tell readers how they should vote. Instead, it offers insights into how they might go about voting in the light of their Christian faith.

Voting: the last thing you should do[8]

Complaining about politics and politicians is an international sport but in the UK we have it down to a fine and uniquely unproductive art. Unlike in the Middle East, where disaffection prompted the riots and regime changes of the Arab Spring, or the United States, where there is a long (if now declining) tradition of diverse political and civic engagement, in the UK our discontent tends to manifest itself most readily in a kind of passive–aggressive grumble. The standard response to complaints about politicians or problems of local or national government is to ask whether the complainer voted – the implication being that if those complaining didn't then they have no right to object (in fact, this national meme once formed the basis of a public information film). The standard response to *that* question is that there's no point voting: because a single vote won't make any difference, because the parties are all the same and because nothing ever changes, anyway.

Both the question and its answers betray a misunderstanding of what 'engagement' in the political process means. Consumerism is our culture's guiding ideology. We are used to having choice without effort, of changing the world around us in order to suit our desires and needs. Whether it's what we consume in terms of TV, music and other media, the clothes we wear, the coffee we drink, our mobile phone, the company we keep – the message is that we get what we want, our way. We are used to instant gratification at the press of a button. We are not used to working slowly and patiently towards a goal.

Ticking a box on a ballot paper is the ultimate form of consumer-ready political engagement: simple, fast and low-effort (and even then many of us can't be bothered to visit the polling station – roll on voting by text message, *X Factor* style). However, our consumerism-conditioned minds mean that we typically load on to this one brief act our entire expectations for political transformation over the course of the next parliament. This is, of course, entirely unrealistic. If we believe our participation in politics begins and ends on Election Day, no wonder voters feel so distant from government.

Disengaging vs making a difference

Of course, there are plenty of reasons, or rather excuses, to disengage. As we have seen, the media is responsible for a continual drip-feed of disparaging news about politicians: the expenses scandal, cash for questions, cash for access, affairs and sleaze of all kinds and, of course, the farcical nature of Prime Minister's Question Time, which accounts for a tiny percentage of most MPs' time but a large proportion of their public image. Nothing surprises us any more. We have grown used to the tabloid stories that constitute our largest source of information about what our government representatives apparently get up to.

Dig just a little below the surface, though, and you find that the reality is very different. We happily tar all of our politicians with the same brush used for the corrupt or careless few, but when we're asked about our local MP the story is often one of patient and hard work on the day-to-day issues that matter most to the community. A small number may be untrustworthy, lazy or in it for self-advancement – just as a small percentage of police, teachers, GPs and church leaders are, too. Most, however, do an excellent job under very difficult circumstances.

The awkward reality is that the problems won't be solved by moaning from the sidelines. But making a difference takes an effort: armchair criticism is far easier than constructive activism. The good news is that, contrary to popular belief, political participation is not a binary decision between representing a constituency as an MP and voting at a General Election every five years.

There is a quote attributed to Joseph Stalin: 'History is made by those who turn up.' Whatever the flaws in his politics, it's hard to deny that Stalin was on the money with this one. You can't expect to have influence if you don't get involved in some way.

Herein lies the tension in this book: *Votewise 2015* is published ahead of the General Election, but in using that opportunity to open a discussion about how we think about the issues most important to us, there is the risk of reinforcing the mistaken assumption that voting is synonymous with political engagement. It is not. There are many ways that we can get involved, and may already be involved. Just some of these include the following.

• Participate in a local election campaign, as well as voting in your local election.
• Join a political party.
• Become a councillor.
• Become a school governor.
• Join a trade union.
• Get involved with pressure groups and think tanks.

- Write to your MP.
- Better still, attend MP's or councillors' surgeries.
- Pray.

Luton South

In fact, however you choose to get involved, you will often find that if you show a basic level of diligence and willingness you will be ahead of most of the competition and will invite further responsibility. All the major parties are short of local supporters and welcome new interest.

Andy Flannagan, Director of Christians on the Left, relates the story of Gavin Shuker, who was elected Labour MP for Luton South in 2010: 'Gavin was born and grew up in Luton. He went to his local comprehensive school and won a scholarship to Cambridge to study Social and Political Sciences. During his time at university he experienced a strong call back home to plant a new church out of his church in Cambridge. He managed to convince around ten other Cambridge graduates to come with him back to Luton in 2006, where they founded a small church with a vision for building a community among unchurched people in the area.

'As part of their mission, some of the group joined the local Labour Party. They were much younger than the average party member, and brought new enthusiasm and ideas with them. As a result of his leadership and communication skills, Gavin was soon given the task of organizing the website and managing the local party's database. He then gained a part-time job working with Margaret Moran, who was the MP at the time. Margaret Moran stood down and was later barred from running again as the Labour MP in the 2010 election after her expenses claims prompted widespread anger from the public and press. Gavin decided to stand as the Labour candidate instead and was ultimately selected after a close battle with another local party member. In May 2010, he was elected as the Labour MP for Luton South at the age of 28.'

This remarkable story shows what can happen when Christians with a vision act together. Key to Gavin's success was that he was backed by a group of people who shared that vision for a local community. Not all of us will be MPs, but we often choose not to get involved owing to obstacles that, in the event, don't exist. Andy Flannagan continues: 'The key to Gavin's success was not simply his winsome engagement, but the fact that this was an adventure that a community of people went on together. As I spent time with them during the campaign, I was continually amazed by how others joined in the adventure, and these folks were drawn from all manner of backgrounds. They were drawn to something of the kingdom. Relationships between Christians and Muslims, believers and non-believers were forged in a way that simply would not have been possible otherwise.'

Your kingdom come?

Many of us will question whether getting involved in politics – at any level – is really worth it. We may be highly active in our churches, doing good work with various organizations in the community, and lack the time to devote to another cause. This work might be acutely needed – debt counselling, action against poverty, work with the marginalized. It can seem far more important and worthwhile *now* than engaging with a political process that can be long, tedious and bureaucratic, and may or may not bear fruit at some point in the future.

Valuable as it is, much of this work addresses symptoms. We also have a responsibility to look for the causes and change them. As Desmond Tutu said, 'As Christians, we need to not just be pulling the drowning bodies out of the river. We need to be going upstream to find out who is pushing them in.' Although the political process can sometimes be agonizingly slow and frustrating, it does bring about real change and is a strand of transformation we cannot afford to overlook. The Old Testament prophets spoke to the heart of power and sought to influence national policy at its source, as well as delivering their challenge

to the people of Israel: their grassroots campaigns were comple-
mented by their critique of official attitudes.

This question also reflects an important aspect of our faith.
Do we see this world as a temporary, throwaway realm – one
in need of palliative care but that will ultimately be replaced –
or one that cries out for redemption in its current form? To
put it another way, when we think of God's kingdom, is it a
disembodied realm in the sky or heaven on earth? The latter
is surely more faithful to the Bible's message: Jesus taught us
to pray 'Your kingdom come on earth as it is in heaven', not
'Your kingdom come in heaven instead of on earth'. His par-
ables were full of physical, earthly imagery like yeast spreading
through dough and seeds bearing fruit in the field: of heaven
taking hold on earth, now imperfectly and partially but one day
fully. Revelation speaks of a 'new earth', but the Greek word
suggests one that is renewed or restored, not replaced to start
again from scratch.[9]

The last thing you should do

Election Day brings both an opportunity and a problem. The
opportunity is that this is arguably the easiest way for us to participate in the political process and to make a real and tangible
difference to the way our country is run and the ideas that shape
policymakers' decisions. The problem is that it is also easy to
place a cross on our ballot sheet and to use this as an excuse to
disengage from politics for the next five years.

For Christians, engaging with politics has to go beyond the
ballot box. Voting is not the be-all and end-all. In fact, it should
be the last thing we do in the course of a parliament: the final
act of our engagement up to the election and the expression of
our ongoing participation rather than the extent of it. So as we
think through the issues and try to decide which party to vote
for, we need to remember that this isn't a one-day-only event.
The argument that a single vote won't make any difference may
be right. But the real challenge for Christians is not choosing

the right party and giving them our one vote. It's deciding on a party or an issue to support and sticking with it, both for Election Day itself and the 1,825 days before the next one.

Marriage and family

Unlike in the United States, there is no strong Christian vote in the UK. The Anglican Church gained a tongue-in-cheek reputation as the 'Tory Party at prayer' sometime back in the eighteenth century, and this perception has vaguely persisted ever since. Not without reason: at least until the last election, some 45 per cent of professing Anglicans did indeed vote Conservative. This is not a majority, but it still represents the largest slice of Anglican voters. But no political party appeals to Christians as a whole more than another. Christians of any denomination can and do support any of the main parties.

One of the reasons for this lack of polarization is that in the UK there are few deal-breakers for Christian voters. In the USA, the correlation between voting intention and the Christian faith results from voters coalescing around a handful of watershed issues, including abortion and the free market. In the UK, such issues don't tend to provoke the public to vote one way or another – partly because the lack of stark distinctions between the parties on these issues means that there would be no natural home for them. (Incidentally, Christians in the UK generally sit towards the left of the political spectrum, even if they tend to the right on moral issues. 'If you analyse Christian opinion in the UK, they are more likely to be left-leaning in their economic persuasions. For instance, 64% say they believe the government should provide a decent standard of living for the unemployed. That would be complete anathema to the US Religious Right.')[10] In any case, Christians are not seen as a force to be harnessed by one or other political party.

Same-sex marriage

However, if there is now one issue that has motivated – or rather demotivated – Christians in the course of the last parliament, it is gay marriage. The move to legalize same-sex marriage prompted a huge grassroots campaign supported by a wide range of Christian groups as well as members of the public who were socially conservative but would not describe themselves as religious. The policy was supported by the Conservative, Liberal Democrat and Labour leadership, though Conservative MPs were given a free vote and more than half of the party's MPs voted against it. UKIP opposed the bill on the grounds that it was illiberal and the power of the European Court of Human Rights would lead to religious groups being forced to perform same-sex marriages against their consciences.

While UKIP has seen some increase in popularity as a result, the greater effect has been for Christians to desert in droves the parties they once supported. Rather than find a brand new party to stand behind (and UKIP is the only real choice), it is more likely that many Christians will simply not vote at all in the 2015 election. Turnout is already likely to be low for the reasons described earlier. Same-sex marriage has given many socially conservative voters, including a large number of Christians, a strong incentive to stay at home. They feel, not without cause, that their politicians do not listen to them and do not represent their interests. The Conservatives stand to suffer the most, with one survey showing that they risk losing 57 per cent of church-going Christians who previously voted for them.[11]

Pro-marriage?

David Cameron made a point of explaining his support for same-sex marriage as part of his wider concern for family stability. At the 2011 Conservative conference he argued: 'Conservatives believe in the ties that bind us; that society is stronger when we make vows to each other and support each other. So I don't support gay marriage despite being a Conservative. I support gay marriage because I am a Conservative.'

Marriage has long been a prominent theme of Conservative Party policy. In 2010 David Cameron promised to make his government the most family-friendly ever, a promise that Labour were quick to point out had been broken by the coalition's cuts to Child Tax Credits and other benefits. Much has been made of the so-called 'couple penalty', the bias in the tax system against low-paid married couples with children versus their unmarried counterparts. Plans for a transferable tax allowance to address this were delayed due to the austerity agenda but have been reinstated for 2015–16. The tax break of up to £200 for some couples drew criticism from the opposition, with Shadow Chief Secretary to the Treasury Rachel Reeves claiming: 'He's so out of touch he thinks people will get married for £3.85 a week.'

Why family?

Most of our knowledge of marriage and divorce in the Bible is indirect. This likely reflects the fact that marriage was so common it was generally regulated by well-known custom – hence no wedding ceremony is systematically described. However, because that custom was so widespread there is a large amount of material in the Bible, both about the marriage process and the significance of marriage.[12]

In the Bible, marriage and family (the two are, unsurprisingly, inextricably linked in biblical thought) are treated as fundamentally important to the health and success of the Jewish nation and protected in every strand of law. Whether it is the regulations surrounding military service, property ownership, Sabbath observance or permitted sexual relationships, marriage and the family were considered sacrosanct. Sexual order is foundational to relational order, and a prerequisite for a strong society.[13]

The reason for this is that the Bible recognizes that our lives are interconnected. We cannot deal with one element of society – employment, government, finance, criminal justice, welfare, and so on – in isolation from the others.[14] Trying to fix a problem in one area without understanding this creates a series of side effects:

> Like bubbles under the wallpaper, if we push one down it often leads to unintended consequences elsewhere. Policies that affect employment also impact couples and family structure, since they influence who works where, for how long, and for how much money. Family structure affects the welfare budget, which picks up the costs of broken and struggling households. Interest rates impact unemployment, but they also affect how much families pay on their mortgages and credit cards and the financial problems or freedom they experience as a result.[15]

The extended family was the setting within which the Israelites taught their children God's laws and brought up the next generation of faithful followers. It was the context of land ownership and economic independence. It was the basis of the welfare system and the foundation of community life and local government. Without strong and cohesive extended families, Israelite society would crumble.

Family under fire

In our culture, the nuclear family rather than the extended family is the basic unit of society. Moreover, even the nuclear family has suffered in recent years. This appears to be linked to marriage rates; families with married parents are more likely to stay together in the long term. Family breakdown is also strongly associated with poverty. The Centre for Social Justice, an influential centre-right think tank, has carried out extensive work in this area:

> We did a report into the state of the nation and why family breakdown is such a problem in the UK today. Half of all

children born today will not still be with both their parents by the time they're 15 and marriage is a more durable relationship . . . Ninety-three per cent of all couples still together by the time the child is 15 are married.[16]

The organization identifies a cluster of five interrelated and mutually reinforcing 'pathways to poverty': family breakdown, educational failure, worklessness and dependency, addiction and serious personal debt.[17]

There is a huge personal and public cost to family breakdown: one that affects us all. As something that is of such fundamental importance in the Bible and to our own society, Christians are right to be concerned about the state of family life and marriage. The question is how we express that concern.

Hummus and same-sex marriage

American comedian and Democratic Senator Al Franken writes, 'Asking whether there is a liberal or conservative bias to the mainstream media is a little like asking whether al Qaeda uses too much oil in their hummus. The problem with al Qaeda is that they're trying to kill us.'[18] His point is that while there is arguably a degree of liberal bias in certain areas of the media, this is dwarfed by other, far more significant and dangerous biases. 'Most of these biases stem from something called "the profit motive." This is why we often see a bias toward the Sensational . . . Pack Mentality. Negativity. Soft News. The Don't-Offend-the-Conglomerate-That-Owns-Us bias. And, of course, the ever-present bias of Hoping There's a War to Cover.'

Same-sex marriage is far from a trivial issue. We do not know what its impacts will be. Nevertheless, it is just the latest of many far-reaching ways in which marriage and family have been redefined over the last few decades. In this sense, it is a symptom of changing mores and a catalyst for further change, not a root cause in itself. Since the 1960s, the marriage rate has dropped by half, divorce rates have doubled, and cohabitation before marriage has overwhelmingly become the norm. By 2016 more children will be born outside marriage than within it.[19] Complaining about same-sex marriage while overlooking these other changes is, in Al Franken's words, a little like asking whether al Qaeda uses too much oil in their hummus. Certainly, we need to address the erosion of marriage and family life in the UK, and the Church is well placed to do that. Continuing to engage with the government on same-sex marriage may be one aspect of that process for Christians who feel led to be active in that area. But focusing on same-sex marriage to the exclusion of all the other ways in which marriage and family have changed over the last 50 years risks overlooking far greater threats to family stability. At the very least, same-sex marriage must be understood and addressed within this wider context.

The bottom line

Surveys suggest that Christians are divided on the same-sex marriage issue, with active churchgoers more likely to oppose it.[20] Vast anecdotal evidence and commentary, as well as polling,[21] show that introducing same-sex marriage has been a prime vote loser for the Conservative Party.

Many Christians feel that the coalition government's decision to push the same-sex marriage bill through parliament was undemocratic and will use this as an excuse to disengage from political activity. However, it is worth bearing in mind that 161 MPs voted against the bill at its final reading. (The lists of who voted for and against can be found online.)[22] Furthermore, by disengaging we necessarily cease to have any influence. Despite the frustrations of ostensibly being ignored by our government, we cannot change things by opting out. In fact, by getting involved now, when levels of political engagement are at an all-time low, we have a greater opportunity than ever to make a difference.

Points for action

- Remain involved: do not use same-sex marriage as a reason to disengage from either voting or (ideally) wider political activity.
- Find out your own MP's views on marriage and the importance of family life, and the views of prospective MPs in your constituency.
- If 'time is the currency of relationships', how can you re-organize your own time to invest more with family and the relationships that matter the most to you?

2

UK plc

A vision for the future (what's the economy for?)

'It's the economy, stupid.' Bill Clinton's 1992 election campaign catchphrase has even more relevance for us today. Since the financial crisis of 2008 the economy has dominated headlines and 'getting the economy back on track' has become a litmus test of political competence. The Conservatives advocate a programme of continuing austerity to avoid bankrupting the country, claiming that Labour's profligate borrowing during the boom years led to unsustainable public debt. Labour say that a growing economy would better allow us to pay down our debts, and that the Conservatives' irresponsible cuts to the public sector are slowing the recovery. The Lib Dems are keen to ensure that the poorest are shielded from the worst of the effects of the recession and the measures used to fix it.

With the economy apparently turning a corner in 2013, the Conservatives claim that 'the medicine is working'. Yet the road remains rocky, and the effects of high inflation for some time means that it may be several more years before households feel any better off than they did before the last election – allowing Labour to sidestep the technicality of economic growth and recast the problem as a 'cost of living crisis'. Whoever is right, of all the policies the different parties unveil and the principles behind them, it is confidence in their ability to manage the economy that will win them the most votes.

The economy, stupid?

We have made economic growth our overriding goal. Ipsos MORI polls consistently show the economy as the most important issue facing the country today.[1] The party that delivers growth, or delivers the clearest and most promising plan for it, will probably win the election.

A question we only rarely ask is what the economy is *for*.

GDP – gross domestic product – is the sum total of the country's economic activity. The government points to rising GDP as evidence of economic recovery, with some justification: by definition, rising GDP means that the country is out of recession. But that doesn't mean GDP alone is a helpful measure of economic activity. GDP *per capita* – economic activity averaged for each individual in the country – will take much longer to recover than overall GDP, which has partly been driven by a growing population. Household incomes remain squeezed.

More importantly, our focus on GDP ignores the question of whether economic activity itself is a worthwhile goal. As Bobby Kennedy said in 1968:

> Too much and too long, we seem to have surrendered community excellence and community values in the mere accumulation of material things. Our gross national product – if we should judge America by that – counts air pollution and cigarette advertising, and ambulances to clear our highways of carnage. It counts special locks for our doors and the jails for those who break them. It counts the destruction of our redwoods and the loss of our natural wonder in chaotic sprawl. It counts napalm and the cost of a nuclear warhead, and armored cars for police who fight riots in our streets. It counts Whitman's rifle and Speck's knife, and the television programs which glorify violence in order to sell toys to our children.[2]

GDP evaluates everything but knows the value of nothing: 'the health of our children, the quality of their education, or the joy of their play ... the beauty of our poetry or the strength of our marriages; the intelligence of our public debate or the integrity of our public officials'. These things cannot be measured financially.

Politicians talk a lot about the economy. Ask politicians what the *purpose* of economic activity is, though, and they are harder pressed to give a good answer. The purpose is not ever-increasing GDP: GDP is what economic activity *is*, not what it's *for*. It's not job creation, though the employment figures are almost as closely watched as those for GDP. It's worth mentioning that the Bible has a high opinion of work: we are called to wise stewardship of the resources we have been given. Adam's task was to work and take care of the Garden of Eden (Genesis 2.15) and the Bible sees employment as a vital part of engaging with society. Consequently no one should be consigned to worklessness. But economic activity is not an end in itself – and nor are the wages employment provides.

When we discuss the economy, we need to bear in mind that we're really talking about something quite different. The purpose of economic activity is not economic activity itself: it is the opportunities for such things as safety, belonging, consumption, leisure, status and identity that jobs and money provide. The ultimate goal of economic activity is something far less tangible than GDP, and far harder to measure. Secular thinkers might express this in different ways, including 'happiness' or perhaps the more all-encompassing (and less hedonistic) term 'well-being'. While well-being starts to hint at the real aim, it is the biblical idea of *shalom* that truly informs us here. *Shalom* is a state of completeness that is reflected in every area of life, from the economic and material to the relational and spiritual.

Can't buy me love . . .

From our culture's secular viewpoint, then, the purpose of the economy might be to create and distribute wealth in a way that maximizes society's happiness and welfare. This is a shadow of the vision offered by the biblical concept of *shalom*, but even this points to the economy being about far more than money. Different approaches have tried to achieve that end in different ways, typically by taking economic planning and major industries into state control for the benefit of all (communism) or by relaxing control of the markets and industry and allowing the laws of supply and demand to allocate resources most effectively (capitalism). But in the end, the question is not what they are trying to achieve, but how and why.

The saying goes that money can't buy happiness, but it can buy a better class of misery. What we tend to find in reality is that money *does* bring a degree of happiness – it's hard to be happy without the basic security of food, safety and shelter – but that we rapidly reach a point of diminishing returns. Someone who earns £250,000 a year is unlikely to be ten times happier (whatever that means) than someone on £25,000.

Adjusted for inflation, GDP per capita has risen around four-fold since the Second World War. Levels of happiness as assessed by surveys have declined. Typical indicators for unhappiness have either risen enormously (like crime and alcohol consumption) or not changed appreciably (like suicide rates) since then. At some point, happiness became decoupled from material prosperity. Studies show that above the poverty threshold, wealth has less and less effect on increasing our well-being.[3] Money is a poor proxy for happiness.

Part of the reason is that we have been pursuing 'prosperity' the wrong way. What we call economic growth has largely been driven by a massive surge in debt – government, personal and corporate (see further in the next section). This kind of economic expansion is not financially sustainable. Neither is it environmentally sustainable. Economic growth rests on our intensive use of natural resources and high rates of consumption. Lastly, it is not socially sustainable. We work long hours, commute long distances and bring our jobs home with us. Like money, time is subject to an opportunity cost: we cannot spend the same minute or the same pound twice. Chasing happiness by means of economic growth tends to come at the expense of the things that really make us happy: our relationships.

The root of all kinds of evil?

Contrary to popular belief, the Bible is not against the pos-
session of wealth *per se*. Abraham was a very rich man. Several
women of independent means supported Jesus in his ministry.
Joseph of Arimathea, who gave his own tomb for Jesus' burial,
was a wealthy Jewish leader. What characterizes all these people
and others is that they were righteous, and their wealth did not
prove a distraction from living lives that honoured God. The
prosperous woman in Proverbs 31 is praised not just for her hard
work but because she 'opens her arms to the poor and extends
her hands to the needy'.

The Bible does not view money as inherently evil, though
it is something that comes with vehement warnings attached.
There are a handful of wealthy characters in the Bible who did
not allow their riches to corrupt them. Far more frequent is the
criticism of those who amass riches by injustice – a common
theme for the prophets – and overlook the responsibilities to
the poor and needy that wealth brings with it. Jesus graphically
illustrated the tension between wealth and righteousness when
he said that it is easier for a camel to go through the eye of a
needle than for a rich man to enter the kingdom of God.

So, money is a tool, but a dangerous one that has a habit of
mastering us. Throughout both Testaments, the pursuit of material riches is presented in serious tension with the pursuit of
God's will. As Matthew 6.24 reads: 'No one can serve two mas-
ters. Either you will hate the one and love the other, or you
will be devoted to the one and despise the other. You cannot
serve both God and Money.' Like anything, when we give it
precedence over God it becomes an idol. 'For the love of money
is a root of all kinds of evil. Some people, eager for money,
have wandered from the faith and pierced themselves with many
griefs' (1 Timothy 6.10).

The question is how we harness this tool for the good of
society, rather than turning it into an idol by elevating it as a goal

or a measure of happiness in its own right. And this is where the Bible has something truly revolutionary to offer.

Joined-up thinking

We have latched on to economic activity as a proxy for happiness, and politicians are keen to deliver it at almost any cost. Yet chasing GDP growth doesn't just risk overlooking other aspects of society to their detriment: it ensures it.

This is the way politics is increasingly moving. The days of the grand vision are gone. What tends to engage people nowadays is specific issues, be they outlawing fox-hunting, giving retired Gurkhas the right to settle in the UK, addressing high energy prices or protesting against the latest war in the Middle East. The result is a mass of single-issue campaigns, and parties that react to the disparate concerns of voters on an almost day-by-day basis. Worse, parties' policies not only lack coherence, but they can pull in different directions. No area of life exists in isolation, after all.

The Bible has a very different vision. It is a vision in which the component parts of society work towards the same ends. Those ends – summarized by Jesus in Matthew 22 as the purpose of all of the Law and the Prophets – are love for God and love for neighbour. Love, of course, is not a measure of economic progress. It is a quality of relationship. Every law in the Old Testament aimed to bring about or maintain right relationships, in one or more areas of life.

This means that some of the things we take for granted were supposed to look very different to the Israelites. The overriding aim was to foster and maintain the networks of relationships that provide support, identity and well-being for all of us. All of the different components of society worked in parallel for this end, rather than any one of them being elevated above the others, and above that concern for strong, healthy relationships.

The foundations of this 'joined-up vision' can be found in Leviticus 25, one of the less-read passages of the less-read

Testament. Its aims are so radical that they prompted one political economist to write, 'Leviticus Chapter 25 is a passage that makes *Das Kapital* look tame.'[4] The chapter speaks of debt being cancelled every seven years; land that had been sold being returned to its original families every 50 years; slaves (essentially long-term labourers in Israelite society, unlike the no-holds-barred slavery of neighbouring countries like Egypt and Assyria) periodically being freed to return to their homes – none of which seem to have much relevance to our twenty-first century, capitalism-conditioned minds. But the effects of these laws were intended to determine the shape and nature of the communities in the land of Israel.

Strong families and communities are fundamental to the stability of society as a whole: stability we have badly undermined in a multitude of ways, with steep costs that encompass the financial as well as the emotional and relational. Instead of being recognized as important, strong family, community and stakeholder relationships have received little support or investment in public policy – let alone being a deliberate goal. Unsurprisingly, the impact of the Jubilee legislation also went far beyond the financial realm.

For example, we are used to seeing property as an asset of (hopefully) ever-appreciating value. There is a discussion over whether rising house prices are a good thing (because they fuel economic growth) or a bad one (because they price some people out of the market). The Bible doesn't see property as an asset to be permanently bought and sold at all. By ensuring that every household had access to a piece of land at least once in everyone's lifetime, it gave families long-term roots in an area and a measure of economic independence. Families were more likely to stay together rather than being fragmented by the need to find work elsewhere – and were thus better able to care for each other.

The same goes for the laws that governed debt and employment. The expansion of our economy is fuelled by debt, including mortgage debt. The Bible's intention is that no one should be forced into a cycle of perpetual debt, with no chance of escape (see further in the next section). We chase economic activity with near 24/7 work and shopping. Biblical laws about the importance of resting from work on the Sabbath meant that even low-paid workers were protected from exploitation by the wealthy, as well as having time to spend with their families, and to worship God. Economic activity was integrated into the need for strong family and community relationships, rather than competing with them.

The bottom line

Politicians often talk about a 'balanced economy', meaning one in which no sector is disproportionately represented – without acknowledging that the economy is about far more than numbers in an accounts ledger. It is about balanced, integrated lives. The purpose of the economy is to allow citizens to participate fully in society, enabling them to engage in the activities and relationships that best promote their well-being. The way the economy is managed, and even the assumptions politicians and the public make about the purpose of the economy, fundamentally affects their ability to do that. Understanding what the different parties are ultimately trying to achieve gives us a way to evaluate their strategies of raising taxes, cutting interest rates, and otherwise working to foster economic growth.

Points for action

- Do you see a vision behind the different parties' economic policies, or is unquestioned economic growth simply the end in itself?
- Is stewardship of the economy integrated with other factors, such as maintaining a home life, limiting working hours, addressing unmanageable debt, and creating opportunity for all?
- What role does economic activity play in shaping your own networks of relationships?

Debt, deficit and austerity

Like many countries, the UK has a love–hate relationship with debt. Like an alcoholic who has recognized that our drinking is fast approaching catastrophic levels, we have decided that we urgently need to do something about the amount we are borrowing. Just not quite yet.

We have already begun to explore themes of debt in the previous section, but the sheer scale of public and private debt in the UK and its dominance in the backdrop to the 2015 election warrants in-depth exploration. **National debt** – the total money the government has borrowed over the years – is approaching 100 per cent of GDP. The **deficit**, or the amount of money the government has to borrow in a year to make up its spending shortfall (and which is added to the long-term national debt), topped £159 billion for 2009–10, before falling somewhat in subsequent years. However, Chancellor George Osborne's aspiration to eliminate the deficit by the end of the parliament has proved unrealistic. Austerity will have to continue well into the next parliament before the total debt even stops growing. After that, we still have to pay the interest on the public debt, which will cost us more than £70 billion annually by 2018.

Personal debt is also eye-wateringly high. Including mortgages, personal debt totals more than £1.4 trillion – again roughly equal to GDP. Unsecured lending or consumer credit stands at around £160 billion. Including mortgage debt, we owe around £29,000 for every adult in the country: more than an entire year's income for the average person.[5] And, as we explored above, debt is intrinsically linked to economic growth – one reason that politicians are wary when they talk about its evils. David Cameron had to rewrite one conference speech that appeared to advise voters to pay down their credit card debts, something that would have crushed the recovery if it had been taken literally. Not that we have the money, nationally or individually, to pay off our loans. Of course, not paying them off costs us even more in the long run.

To say that we have a problem with debt is to understate the matter.

What is debt for?

The previous section in this chapter asked what the purpose of economic activity is, and contrasted this with the Bible's approach. With debt, too, we see a gulf between the views of the Bible and those of contemporary culture.

We go into debt when there is no choice; the frantic debt-funded bailouts of failing banks in 2008 are one of the best examples of this. But we also go into debt because we want to. Public and private debt have both ballooned in the last 20 years. A part of that is because recession and rising prices have forced us to borrow money to make ends meet. But a part is simply down to choice. Both government and household spending increased during the boom years, when people might reasonably have been expected to pay down existing debts. There is a reasonable argument that borrowing rose *because* of a thriving economy, which pushed up asset prices and forced down interest rates, making borrowing both more necessary and simultaneously more affordable. But the result is the same: we now have unsustainable levels of debt. The interest payments take a sizeable chunk of our personal and national income. If interest rates rise, as they surely must sooner or later, some of those payments will become even less affordable.

Taking out a loan is a way of bringing forward future spending power to today: if we can't afford something now, we can borrow against future earnings. This, after all, is how most of us buy a house. Securing a mortgage is the only way to access the kind of money we need. The interest payments over many years mean that we might end up paying twice as much as the sum borrowed, but that is just the price we pay for owning our own home. For most people, there is no good alternative. But add to that the credit card debt, store cards, unsecured loans, overdrafts and other forms of lending – it may be that we genuinely can't afford to buy what we need to live, but often the case is that we prefer not to wait to purchase something we want.

It's worth noting that we are the first generation in history to view debt as a convenience, as well as a necessity. Until recently, going into debt has been viewed as a major undertaking, bringing with it serious obligations to repay the loan. For us, as debt has become ever easier to access, so too have bankruptcy proceedings. We no longer think it a serious matter to go into debt, and neither do we worry too much about defaulting. After all, if whole countries can default on their national debt worth hundreds of billions of pounds, why shouldn't individuals default on a few thousand pounds? In October 2013 the USA, the world's largest economy, came within hours of being unable to pay its creditors due to seemingly intractable political divisions. Flirting with default of that magnitude does not set a good example to the citizens who have to pay for those debts, and their own.

Debt and default in the Bible

Unsurprisingly, the Bible has a radically different attitude towards debt. Throughout the Bible, the Israelites are warned of the dangers of debt. Proverbs 22.7 warns that 'the rich rule over the poor, and the borrower is slave to the lender'. Debt was a last-ditch solution that people were forced into to avoid absolute destitution, not something they opted for voluntarily. Jesus repeatedly uses debt as an image for sin, not least in the Lord's Prayer: 'forgive us our debts, as we also have forgiven our debtors' (Matthew 6.12).

Just one of the reasons debt was taken so seriously was the absolute obligation to repay a loan. Security was taken for smaller loans (Deuteronomy 24.10). If a debt could not be repaid, the debtor might be sold into slavery (e.g. Exodus 22.3), or if a loan could not be accessed then selling the whole household into servitude was the only way to avoid starvation. However, in Old Testament Israel, these 'slaves' were to be treated as long-term hired labourers (Leviticus 25.39–40, and see the previous section on the economy). Matthew 18.25 shows that the practice was also normal in the Greco-Roman world of the New Testament. Psalm 37.21 is very clear that not repaying your debt is a 'wicked' thing to do. This is because you have not only stolen money from someone, you have also broken your promise. Defaulting breaks two of the Ten Commandments. Romans 13.7–8 stresses Christians' obligations to pay what they owe.

Both debt and default, then, are treated extremely seriously in the Bible. Because of this wariness, debt was carefully regulated in the Old Testament. Charging interest was banned in almost every circumstance. The Israelites were expressly banned from charging their countrymen any interest at all. The one exception was a foreigner from outside Israel. 'Do not charge a fellow Israelite [lit. your brother] interest, whether on money or food or anything else that may earn interest. You may charge a foreigner [Hebrew: *nokrî*] interest, but not a fellow Israelite, so that the Lord your God may bless you in everything you put your hand to in the land you are entering to possess' (Deuteronomy 23.19–20). One reason for this was presumably that someone who was not bound to keep Israel's law could take an interest-free loan and lend it out at profit to someone else.[6]

As well as banning interest, all loans were to be limited for a maximum of seven years. In the seventh year, every loan was to be cancelled. This meant that no one would be kept in long-term poverty, either by large debts or by high interest payments. Coupled with the Jubilee laws that required the return of land to its families of origin every 50 years, the result was that no one would be forced into perpetual debt with no hope of economic freedom. The Jubilee laws also removed inter-generational debt.

We tend to view debt as a tool: one that allows us to access opportunity we might otherwise miss. The Bible also sees debt as a tool, but looks at the other side of the coin: debt is a tool by which the rich extract money from the poor. The Israelite vision was that 'There need be no poor people among you' (Deuteronomy 15.4). Consequently debt had to be managed carefully.

Crossing the void

The Bible's approach to debt and interest looks something between naive and radical when viewed through the lens of twenty-first-century financial practices. How are we to apply these principles to an economy that is built on vast mountains of debt?

The first point is that such enormous levels of debt are entirely unbiblical. We should never have allowed ourselves to get into such serious debt, and extracting ourselves from that situation should be a priority – as politicians and economists agree. The question is not whether but *how* we go about it. There is a dividing line between the Conservatives, who believe we should cut spending to bring down the budget deficit, and Labour, who claim that stimulating growth will increase tax receipts and allow us to pay our debt down. Though the political parties take every opportunity to criticize each other's policies, there is no way of knowing whether a different approach would have brought about faster economic recovery and deficit reduction. In any case, while the Bible does not provide direct support for either strategy, it does emphasize the need both to live within our means and to use our talents productively.

It is clear that, no matter how undesirable debt is, the biblical view is that once a loan has been secured it must be paid back. The seven-year programme of debt cancellation was built into the economic system: it was regular, expected and agreed. While we should put a brake on new debts, we cannot apply this principle to our existing debts today, which were agreed under strict terms. Debts may be forgiven by the creditor, but not by unilateral action by the debtor! The Bible views this as theft.

Default should therefore not be an option – even one to consider. The near-default by the USA in October 2013 should never have happened. The threat of default, which constitutes theft and breach of promise, must not be used as a bargaining chip. The view that default is not a big deal, whether in terms of national or personal debt, is categorically not shared by the Bible.

But default is not the only way we can get out of paying what we owe. Inflation has the effect of eroding debt, making it worth less than it once was and therefore easier to pay back. Thus the government is in a quandary. High inflation is undesirable, since voters suffer from rising prices and the value of savings is eroded. But inflation also has the silver lining of reducing the true value of the national debt. The cost of the Second World War pushed the national debt up to well over twice GDP: far worse than it is now. Within 25 years, high inflation rates rapidly brought down the ratio of debt to GDP to just 50 per cent. The total debt itself actually grew in that period, but its impact was inflated away. This apparently remarkable achievement would, in biblical terms, be viewed as an act of appalling dishonesty, defrauding creditors of the money they are owed.

The same is likely to happen in the twenty-first century. No government in over 300 years has paid down the national debt: inflation and rising GDP have simply made the interest payments easier to meet. The government's 2 per cent inflation target is rarely met, and often significantly exceeded. With negative real interest rates (that is, inflation is higher than interest), the value of our debt is gradually evaporating – but so are our pensions and savings. The government's aim is simply to keep debt 'manageable' as a proportion of GDP. The biblical viewpoint is that it is a sin to defraud your creditors, which in this case include domestic pension funds. Not only do we store up huge debts for our children, but we devalue our own pensions and thereby place a greater burden on them for care.

The bottom line

Few disagree that our immense national debt must be dealt with. Both default and inflation are forms of theft, as far as the Bible is concerned. The only other option is paying what we owe. That is unpopular with voters, since money that could be spent on public services instead goes towards reducing the debt mountain. A recovering economy would make the impact of this easier to bear, though in a stagnant economy it would constitute further austerity. The alternative is, once the deficit is eliminated, to leave our debt as it is and simply pay the interest – the way we have historically approached the problem. But this, too, is still a form of theft: we are pushing the ongoing cost of our mistakes on to future generations.

These are tough times, and they call for tough decisions. As Jesus said in Matthew 6.21, 'where your treasure is, there your heart will be also'. The reverse is also true. Martin Luther is said to have spoken of three types of conversion: that of the head, that of the heart, and finally, that of the wallet. How we deal with our national debt and deficit go to the heart of that challenge to Christians to put our money where our mouth is.

Points for action
- What emphasis do the different parties place on paying down the debt (not just reducing the deficit), versus simply maintaining interest payments and letting overall debt shrink in comparison to rising GDP?
- To what extent do their policies promote irresponsible lending and the continuation of a debt-driven economy, or long-term sustainability?
- Do you have unnecessary personal debt, and if so, how might you reduce it?

Welfare, pensions and benefits

The UK's vast welfare budget is an enormous source of controversy and an even larger source of misunderstanding. For 2014 it totals roughly £256.6 billion. That's over a third of all public spending and nearly a sixth of GDP. In other words, for every £6 that UK plc makes, £1 is spent on welfare.

There are plenty of vocal critics who claim we can't possibly afford to pay this colossal sum. There are equally those who say that cutting welfare spending will hit the most vulnerable in society. The debate has, unhelpfully, been polarized as one between 'strivers and shirkers': those who work hard and pay their taxes, and those who live on benefits at their expense.[7] An often repeated criticism of an overly large welfare state is that people are left to 'rot on benefits', with some households seeing three generations of unemployed.[8]

This is not a useful way to frame the debate, and it's not an accurate one. For starters, that enormous figure of £256.6 billion includes some £144.1 billion of pensions as well as £112.5 billion benefits. Pensions, of course, are paid to those who have retired after a lifetime of working and paying their national insurance contributions. These people can hardly be characterized as shirkers.

Second, a large proportion of the remaining £112.5 billion of benefits are paid not to the unemployed but to those who are in work. Working Tax Credit (the clue is in the title) and its companion Child Tax Credit are paid to some 5 million people, with another 2 million eligible but not claiming. Although long-term unemployment, typically defined as lasting a year or more, has been stubbornly high, the majority of unemployment is still temporary: claiming benefits is a stop-gap while people search for their next job. Not only that, but multi-generational unemployment is extremely rare – the 'three workless generations' line makes a good tabloid headline but it's not backed up by the reality. So the lines are blurred; those who are on benefits are overwhelmingly already in work or actively looking for work, rather than welfare layabouts who fund a life of inactivity with state handouts. The arguments that cutting benefits will impact some of the poorest and hardest working, such as those in minimum wage jobs, are well founded.

Lastly, although welfare spending is undoubtedly high, it's worth bearing in mind that we spend proportionally *less* now than we did 20 years ago. The total welfare bill as a proportion of public spending was roughly the same (around 36 per cent) in 1994 as it is in 2014. But unsurprisingly, since the average age of the population has increased, a far larger proportion of that total is now spent on pensions.

What are we trying to achieve?

So the more we look into the figures, the more it becomes clear that the subject of welfare is beset with misinformation and political soundbites. 'Strivers vs shirkers' is a lazy, reductionist way of looking at welfare.

Yet there's no denying that our welfare bill is huge and that, in the present financial climate, reducing it would be helpful. £256 billion is a colossal sum of money, whatever we spend it on. But often, we don't ask that question: what *are* we spending it on?

Ultimately, benefits of all kinds enable people to live without working, or not to work so much – either because they shouldn't have to (pensions), because they can't for one reason or another (Jobseekers' Allowance, Employment and Support Allowance, Statutory Sick Pay and Maternity Pay), because their existing work does not pay enough (Working Tax Credit) or because we recognize the value of other forms of unpaid activity (Child Tax Credit).[9] The most controversial benefits are the ones that enable working-age people not to work at all: the ones that play into the narrative of strivers and shirkers.

When it comes to asking what all these benefits are ultimately *for*, there is more than one answer. Reducing poverty, particularly child poverty, is an obvious starting point. Tony Blair pledged to eradicate child poverty by 2020 by reforming the tax and benefits system, rehabilitating the concept of welfare that he felt had become tarnished: 'In Beveridge's time the welfare state was associated with progress and advancement. Today it is often associated with dependency, fraud, abuse, laziness. I want to make it once again a force for progress.'[10] Blair recognized that addressing the symptoms of the problem was not enough and aimed to tackle the causes of poverty through these reforms, too, offering 'a hand up not a hand out'. The coalition government's slogans of 'welfare to work' and 'making work pay' continued this theme, with the added incentive that our national bank account is heavily in the red. If people aren't in work and they can be, runs the assumption, then they should be. Welfare should be part of the process by which people lift themselves out of poverty by working. But does even this miss something more fundamental?

Welfare in the Bible

When we look at a problem – particularly one as expensive as the welfare budget – our primary framework for understanding it tends to be financial. Poverty is particularly amenable to this method of analysis; the most obvious symptom of poverty, after all – and sometimes the *only* one that we acknowledge – is not having enough money. Consequently we believe we can fix the problem by spending money on it. One standard definition of poverty, stated in the Child Poverty Act 2010, is having household income of 60 per cent or less of the median (after tax, housing costs and utility bills). In the past, the official figures for poverty that use this measure have occasionally shown significant changes for two reasons: median incomes falling, as happened in 2010–11, and governments having 'perverse incentives' to make welfare payments that pushed households just over the poverty threshold.[11]

Other definitions reflect the idea that there is more to poverty than simply not having enough money to survive. In 2000 the House of Commons Scottish Affairs Committee noted:

There are basically three current definitions of poverty in common usage: absolute poverty, relative poverty and social exclusion. Absolute poverty is defined as the lack of sufficient resources with which to keep body and soul together. Relative poverty defines income or resources in relation to the average. It is concerned with the absence of the material needs to participate fully in accepted daily life. Social exclusion is a new term used by the EU and the Government . . . The Prime Minister described social exclusion as 'A short hand label for what can happen when individuals or areas suffer from a combination of linked problems such as unemployment, poor skills, low incomes, poor housing, high crime environments, bad health and family breakdown'.[12]

This last idea of social exclusion begins to get to the heart of the issue. Although we tend to gravitate towards financial definitions (which are easy to understand and quantify), the way the Bible sees poverty is far broader.

The Bible recognizes that poverty is not merely financial in nature. It is those who are most marginalized in society – 'the alien, the orphan, the widow' – who are also most at risk of material deprivation (Deuteronomy 26.12). In this sense, financial poverty tends to be a symptom of relational poverty. This is why the Bible's approach to welfare does not begin and end with charity or handouts. Although these are an important strand of caring for the vulnerable, the overriding aim is to draw people back into relationship with others and enable them to engage with their communities, rather than poverty pushing them away from their networks of supportive relationships.

The Jubilee Laws in Leviticus 25 exemplify this approach. A range of measures were advocated for helping those who had fallen on hard times, including:

- **Interest-free loans** – these made food and credit available without keeping the recipient in a state of poverty through punitive interest payments.
- **Temporary sale of property** – land could be sold until the next year of Jubilee, when it was returned to the original family so they were not permanently deprived of their means of production.

- **Indentured labour,** where someone who could not support his family would work as a hired labourer for a fixed period of time (rather than being bought as a permanent slave) in return for food and accommodation.

Additionally, there was a system of tithing, and gleaning rights brought further provision. All of these helped people in their immediate circumstances, while allowing them to continue to engage with their communities and work towards financial independence again. This emphasis on remaining a part of the community is explicit: 'If one of your countrymen becomes poor and is unable to support himself among you, help him as you would an alien or a temporary resident, so that he can continue to live among you' (Leviticus 25.35).

The purpose of these welfare provisions was not simply to prevent people from starving. It was to ensure that they could participate in the relationships that gave them their identity and mutual support, rather than forcing people to leave their families and communities and look for work, or else take on an existence as a second-class citizen. Work – be it farming their own land, working for someone else or gleaning – was an important part of this. But it was a means to an end – integration – not the end itself.

Welfare problems

This emphasis on relationships of support provides some fresh insights into the problems of our modern-day welfare state. Whether or not we can afford what we currently pay, in the future the bill is set to rise even further. As the wealthy 'baby boom' generation (those born roughly between 1946 and 1964) retires, they will start to collect their pensions rather than paying taxes – resulting in a greater gap in welfare spending. The government has scheduled to raise the State Pension Age to 68 from the mid 2030s and probably to 70 at some point in the future,[13] but the simple fact is that our welfare system was designed to deal with very different circumstances. When William Beveridge published the report in 1942 that paved the way for the welfare state, average life expectancy was 66 years for men and 71 for women.[14] The working assumption was that the state would need to fund just one year of retirement for men, and 11 for women. More than 70 years later, average life expectancy is well over 80 but retirement ages have not been adjusted to reflect this. Many people can expect to spend a third of their lives in retirement. The resulting gap can only be filled in a limited number of ways, or most likely a combination of ways:

- raising taxes
- higher retirement age
- increased public borrowing
- lower pension payments
- cuts elsewhere.

None of these is politically favourable but the simple maths of the situation means that there is little choice. One way or another we will have to find more money or accept lower levels of financial provision. The latter is more realistic. But this does not mean people need face years of poverty and neglect in retirement.

The reality is that a significant proportion of financial spending goes towards making up a relational deficit. State spending, funded by the taxpayer, has replaced many of the tasks that used to be carried out within our networks of closest relationships, particularly the extended family. Even today, the majority of care for the elderly happens within the family, including by partners who have themselves retired. The relationship is not one-way: grandparents provide an enormous amount of care for grandchildren while parents work. However, the more families fragment due to relationship breakdown and mobility for work, the less these arrangements are possible. Instead, the work of childcare and day-to-day support is 'outsourced' to the state, at enormous cost.

The bottom line

Fixing the welfare system includes recognizing, facilitating and incentivizing the mutual relationships of care that already exist within families, and that many more people would love to undertake if only circumstances permitted. Often, the patterns that make this impossible begin very early, with a choice of university or career far away from our roots. The state has a role to play in enabling people to prioritize these relationships in a way that it currently overlooks.

Points for action

- You will potentially be living with the consequences of your MP's welfare policies for decades – make time to understand them properly!
- 'Strivers and shirkers': how much does this narrative determine the way you think about and engage with the welfare debate?
- What does your 'relational pension' look like? In which relationships do you need to invest more for the long term?

3

The global perspective

Europe

Europe has long been a contentious issue. Ever since the UK joined the European Economic Community in 1973, a proportion of voters and politicians have argued that we should leave. The European project has evolved a lot since then, and the question of EU membership has become sharply more controversial over the course of the last parliament. The sudden rise of UKIP – initially a party of protest formed with the sole purpose of withdrawing from the EU – has pushed the issue squarely into the foreground. Representatives of either side of the argument have had to state their own policy on membership in reaction to this, and the political debate has been polarized as a result. Membership of the EU has become a watershed political issue.

Despite this, there is widespread misunderstanding about our role in the EU and both its benefits and its drawbacks. This is partly due to the complexity of the issue and the many different bodies and overlapping agreements between countries that exist. Three of the most relevant terms are:

European Union (EU) – an economic and political union of member states, including the UK, established by the Maastricht Treaty in 1992. The EU includes the single market, which allows free trade and movement of people, labour, goods and capital between member states under a standardized set of laws. EU policies also affect a number of other areas, including justice, home affairs, agriculture and fisheries.

European Economic Area (EEA) – the wider group of countries (EU member states[1] plus Norway, Iceland and Liechtenstein)

which can participate in the EU's single market without necessarily holding full EU membership. Participating countries
outside the EU have to adopt relevant EU law but have little
influence in the decision-making process. They do not pay to be
a member of the EU, but also receive no funds from EU policies.

Eurozone or Euro Area – the economic and monetary union
of 17 of the 28 EU member states (not including the UK) which
have adopted the euro as their common currency, established on
1 January 1999.

The biggest question is whether the UK keeps the status quo by
remaining in the EU, possibly on renegotiated terms, or leaves
the EU but remains in the EEA. Although in the 1990s Tony
Blair fought hard for the UK to join the euro, the financial crisis
hit the Eurozone hard and there is little popular or political will
to do so now. Neither does complete withdrawal from the EEA
have much support.

The roots of the EU

Although the benefits or otherwise of membership of the EU
are now often discussed in narrow economic terms, its roots
lie in the aftermath of the Second World War, when the first
steps towards European integration were taken to prevent the
possibility of another war between its members. The European
Coal and Steel Community (ECSC) was established in 1951,
with a treaty between Belgium, France, West Germany, Italy, the
Netherlands and Luxembourg. Combining their coal and steel
industries in a common market under the same high authority
was intended to promote economic growth and eliminate the
possibility that any country could independently create weapons
to use against another. These early developments are a reminder
that economic prosperity was sought as a means to peace, rather
than an end in its own right.

Pros and cons

Today, membership of the EU gives the UK free access to the world's largest single market. With over 500 million people and a GDP of £11 trillion, the EU is a larger economy than the USA and Japan combined. The stated goals of the EU are to ensure that the movement of capital, labour, goods and services between its member states is as easy as their movement within them. To achieve this, the barriers to free trade have been removed as much as is possible; border control, differences in taxation and legal standards have been harmonized.

This means a number of things. We have access to trade opportunities denied to non-members; however, businesses are also subject to EU regulation. Freedom of movement means that anyone from the EU can come to live and work in the UK; it also means that UK citizens are free to live and work within much of Europe. It means that we have to pay for membership – our net contribution is some €7.3 billion for 2013, but the real cost is arguably many tens of billions more in expensive policies and productivity lost due to regulation, by some estimates.[2] But it also means that we enjoy the advantages of being a member of the single market. Some of these advantages and disadvantages are hard to assess. Farm subsidies cost shoppers around £3 billion per year, for example, but they also buy us a degree of food security. We export £159 billion of goods to the EU, but they export £44 billion less than this back to us. Which is more important?[3]

EU tensions

The arguments are complex, and different people have different reasons for wanting to stay in or leave the EU. On the whole, the UK's voters would prefer to leave.[4] The main reason for this is immigration: if we were outside the EU we would regain control of our borders and have the ability to cut immigration as much as we wanted. Free movement of labour has stoked tensions between nationalities, as migrants are seen to take jobs that 'rightfully' belong to Brits (see further the next section on immigration).

However, there has been vocal opposition to withdrawal from business leaders, and US and European political leadership. Large businesses argue that EU membership gives us global clout, particularly as a financial centre. Among others, Nissan has questioned its continuing investment in the UK if we leave the EU.[5] In November 2013 the CBI (Confederation of British Industry) published research that stated that EU membership is worth approximately 4 to 5 per cent of UK GDP annually, or between £62 and £78 billion (€73–93 billion): around £3,000 for every household. Small businesses, on the other hand, often report that they struggle with the high cost of complying with EU regulation.

We have lost sight of the original purpose of European integration: peace through cooperation and prosperity. Instead, voters now see it in terms of red tape, as a burden that leads to unfair competition for jobs and benefits. To a large number of people, EU membership has become synonymous with issues of immigration.

Political parties

UKIP has tapped into this sentiment and set the tone for the EU debate. Their core message is straightforward: withdraw from the EU, dump Brussels bureaucracy, and regain control of our borders. As they have gained popular support they have branched out from being a single-issue party to formulate a wider range of policies. They can 'broadly be seen as right wing, with a strong libertarian flavour and a dash of social conservatism',[6] though the party has adopted various policies that don't fit with this description.

It is UKIP's proposals for controlling immigration that have won them voters' greatest support. In the 2014 European elections, UKIP took 27 per cent of the vote and have 24 MEPs, coming ahead of Labour and the Conservatives. The Liberal

Democrats' pro-European stance saw them take less than 7 per cent of the popular vote, and lose all but one of their MEPs.

This has also forced the main parties' hands for the coming General Election and next parliamentary term. If they are to appear relevant, they cannot duck the issue. None of the three main parties supports a 'Brexit' (as a British exit from the EU has been dubbed). As a compromise, the Conservatives have agreed to hold a referendum on membership by 2017, if they win the next election, but David Cameron has said that he would vigorously campaign against leaving the EU. Labour have said that they will hold a referendum only in the event of further significant transfer of powers to the EU, which has generally been interpreted as effectively ruling out a popular vote in the course of the next parliament. The Lib Dems do not support a referendum. All would seek to renegotiate the terms under which we stay in the EU, though it is not at all clear what that would mean in practice, or how successful it would be. The Green Party is critical of the EU's structures and would seek to reform it, and supports a referendum on membership.

Biblical government

The Bible has much to say about immigration (see the next section below). How we understand this critical subject is obviously highly relevant to EU membership. But the Bible also has much to say about the structures of power that govern the relationships between a country's people and its central and local bodies of government.

At different times in its history, Israel had various forms of government. For over 400 years it was a monarchy – first united under Saul, David and Solomon, and then divided into the two kingdoms of Israel and Judah after Solomon's death, when the people rebelled against the forced labour that Rehoboam imposed. Ten tribes separated as the northern kingdom under Jeroboam, with Judah and Benjamin left over as the remainder of the house of David under Rehoboam.

Conflict marked relationships between Israel and Judah, until the northern kingdom was exiled by the Assyrians and essentially ceased to exist. Judah was later attacked by the Babylonians, the Jerusalem Temple destroyed and large numbers of people exiled to Babylon in 597 and 587 BC. In this case, however, the nation not only managed to retain its identity but the period was a formative one for the Jews. Under Cyrus the Great in the mid sixth century, they were allowed to return home from exile and rebuild the Temple. Cyrus allowed the Jews a high degree of religious autonomy, though they were still governed by Persian officials (satraps). Aside from a period of independence in the second and first centuries BC, the Jews remained under foreign rule throughout the days of the Greek and Roman Empires.

Due to the varied circumstances of the Jewish people, it is not possible to talk about 'biblical government' as such: there were many forms of government over the centuries of Israel's history, some of which were firmly rooted in the Torah, others that were imposed by domestic or foreign rulers and did not represent God's will. When we look for biblical insights to inform our understanding of our own structures of government, it is the early years of Israel that are most relevant.

Subsidiarity

Israel began its existence in the land of Canaan as a confederation of tribes without centralized government. Instead, the Torah envisions several different and independent sources of authority, each applying to different areas of life. The spheres they encompassed were the individual, the (extended) family, the clan/community, the Levites, the tribe/region and the nation as a whole.[7]

The different spheres of authority were overlapping, and 'higher' sources did not necessarily take precedence over 'lower' ones. Recently married men were exempt from military service for a year, for example (see Deuteronomy 24.5), recognizing the importance of family life.

In general, responsibility for carrying out a task was given to the smallest appropriate body. Criminal justice was handled by local courts, in each village and town, with only the most difficult cases being passed up to a 'court of appeal'. Education and welfare fell within the remit of the family and village, not the state. Israel did very little as a whole nation; the only time they acted under centralized leadership was when invasion by a foreign power posed a threat that could not effectively be dealt with by smaller, local groups. This early ideal for Israel's government has similarities with the idea of subsidiarity from Catholic Social Teaching, as well as Abraham Kuyper's Sphere Sovereignty.

Centralized government is viewed with scepticism, at best. Throughout the Bible the Israelites experienced the abuse inflicted by foreign empires with harsh and distant rulers: first the Egyptians, then the Assyrians, Babylonians, Greeks and Romans. All of these interfered with their political and religious autonomy and placed an unnecessary burden on the people.

Not only that, but Israel's own monarchy was viewed with caution. Deuteronomy 17.14–20 places a series of restrictions on the king. Unlike the all-powerful god-kings of Egypt and elsewhere in the Ancient Near East, Israel's king was not to amass a fortune or a large personal army. And instead of writing the law and being above it, he was to be subject to the Law – writing his own copy and reading it daily, taking instruction from the Levites. Deuteronomy 17 presents the ideal king as an exemplar of humility and faithfulness.

Israel existed in Canaan for over two centuries without a king. It was the military threat posed by the Philistines at the end of the eleventh century BC, alongside the prospect of weak leadership after the prophet Samuel's death, that prompted the Israelites to demand a king 'to lead us and to go out before us and fight our battles' (1 Samuel 8.20). Samuel warned the Israelites of the price they would pay for a king: forced labour and heavy taxation to support the royal household and military campaigns. Still, the Israelite people disagreed and Samuel anointed

Saul as a result. The accounts of 1 and 2 Kings show that most of Israel's monarchs ignored the restrictions of Deuteronomy 17, and their unfaithfulness led to the Babylonian exile.

The bottom line

Unnecessarily centralized authority comes with warnings attached in the Bible. Instead, the ideal is that political and economic power should be as diffuse as possible: 'Decentralization of power facilitates the widespread participation in political and economic decisions, which is a necessary expression of every person being made in God's image.'[8] This also promotes better relationships, since power imbalances and the resentments they breed are kept to a minimum.

Subsidiarity demands that responsibility be devolved to the lowest appropriate level. Stated like this, the principle is little more than common sense: tasks are to be given to those best placed to carry them out. More centralized authorities should be called upon only when a lower body is unable to achieve the required ends. Otherwise, government ends up as a force that takes initiative and responsibility away from its citizens, accumulating power and forcing them to rely on it for things that they could better do themselves. In the best cases such overcentralized power is distant and interfering; in the worst, it is abusive. From its positive beginnings after the Second World War, the EU now represents this kind of distant, uncaring micromanager to many Brits.

The application for the UK's EU membership is clear, and not particularly profound. There are things that the UK cannot do alone. We live in an era of globalization. Dealing with terrorism, international crime and trade negotiations are all easier when we are part of a global community, not isolated to struggle with them on our own.

But equally, there is plenty that we can and should do ourselves, but do not. There are well-known frustrations of EU membership:

While being part of club [*sic*] of 28 countries inevitably means compromise, there is particular annoyance at the sense of a creeping extension of EU authority – regulating on trivial issues, sometimes counter to the wishes of the UK and its citizens, rather than focusing on the big picture issues like growth, trade and the Single Market . . . Areas where UK firms are frustrated with EU regulation include labour market regulation, highlighted by nearly half of businesses as having had a negative impact – with particular frustrations around the Temporary Agency Workers Directive and Working Time Directive.[9]

This is one of only a few instances in this book where direct, specific application will be made based on biblical principles. Staying in the EU but on renegotiated terms, such that we have greater control over the factors that most influence our citizens, is the preferred outcome. If renegotiation is not an option, matters become more complicated.

Points for action

- In what ways does membership of the EU personally affect you, whether positively or negatively, directly or indirectly?
- Do the different parties make a credible case for their positions on the EU?
- To what extent do you conflate immigration and EU membership, and how much do these affect your voting choices?

Immigration

After the economy, immigration is the top issue that motivates the electorate. Voters almost invariably have strong feelings about migrants. They're vulnerable people who need our help, or highly skilled workers we should be recruiting for the good of the country. Or else they're benefit fraudsters and opportunists who are taking our jobs and overloading our public services.

The expansion of the EEA means that more and more people are able to travel to the UK to seek work, and EU regulations mean that there is very little we can do about it. Reducing net migration from a long-term average of over 200,000 per year to less than 100,000 was a flagship pledge of the Conservative manifesto: a difficult enough undertaking given the number of European migrants, and even that number was too high for many voters.

An unclear picture

Immigration is a subject that is beset by confusion, scaremongering and misinformation – much of it entirely deliberate. Certain sections of the media play on the public's fears and exaggerate the problems of immigration. Different categories of migrant are often blurred together, so that we are not invited to distinguish between terms like 'migrant worker', 'illegal immigrant' and 'asylum seeker'.

Not only that, but the landscape has changed markedly over the last ten years. In 2004 the largest category of migrant was asylum seekers, who accounted for over half of net migration. That is still the impression that some tabloids give today. But now, economic migrants and foreign students form by far the largest categories – over two-thirds, between them – while asylum seekers are only 3 or 4 per cent of the total. Popular perceptions might be years out of date. The accession of the EU8 countries[10] swelled the numbers of economic migrants, and the decision to remove all restrictions on migrants from Bulgaria and Romania in 2014 prompted renewed fears. (In fact, the number of Bulgarian and Romanian migrants dropped in the months after the restrictions were lifted, though it still rose over the year as a whole.[11]) We are highly wary of opening our borders to more people. At the same time, there is growing public awareness of the darker side of immigration: those who are trafficked, or who come here illegally and are exploited by ruthless employers.

What's in a name?

The government's categorization of long-term migrants (not counting tourists, who stay for only a short time) is broadly based on their entry route. The categories include economic migrants, students, asylum seekers, family members who join someone already here, and 'illegal' immigrants. This last category is a catch-all term for those whose visas have expired, or whose asylum application has been denied but who have not yet left, or who entered the country illegally. It is also a loaded term, since it implies that they never had any right to be here. We prefer the term 'irregular immigrant', similar to the French 'sans papiers'.

In addition to these five categories, there is the complication of EU membership. Freedom of movement within the EU means that people can travel to the UK for any reason. Migrants from the wider EEA might be students, economic migrants, family members, or none of these. They will never, by definition, be refugees or irregular immigrants.

We have at least five categories of immigrant, though all too often we do not distinguish between them. Broadly speaking, the Bible has just two categories of immigrant. Instead of looking at where they come from or the reasons for their arrival (economic, persecution), the Israelites' response was supposed to be determined by the migrants' circumstances and attitudes.

Immigrants in the Bible

A number of words are used to describe the relationship the Israelites had with those within and outside their borders, though they boil down to just three different statuses: the native-born, the 'resident alien' and the true foreigner.

The *'ezrāḥ* is the native-born Israelite, though in the light of Exodus 12.38 (which describes the Exodus group as a 'mixed multitude', 'great rabble' or, in one translation, 'ethnically diverse crowd') it seems that this could never have been a purely ethnic distinction. After the entry into Canaan it might have referred to someone who was born in the land and into one of the families of Israelites: someone with roots back to the conquest.

The most often mentioned category of immigrant in the Hebrew Bible is the *gēr* (plural *gērîm*), often translated as '[resident] alien' or, more archaically, 'sojourner'. This covers a range of immigrants, but they all are associated with other dependent groups: the hired worker, the poor, widows, orphans and the Levite. These are people without their own land and property who are disproportionately vulnerable; the Law and Prophets warn repeatedly against mistreating them.

'Do not oppress the widow or the fatherless, the alien [*gēr*] or the poor. In your hearts do not think evil of each other' (Zechariah 7.10). The *gēr*'s inclusion with other groups who are vulnerable to economic injustice (the orphan, widow, and poor) supports the chief meaning of 'oppress' here as 'extort'. Having known injustice and oppression themselves, the Israelites were not to mistreat them: 'The alien [*gēr*] living with you must be treated as one of your native-born [*'ezrāḥ*]. Love him as yourself, for you were aliens in Egypt. I am the LORD your God' (Leviticus 19.34). The New Testament picks up this analogy of the Jews being aliens themselves: Christians are 'aliens and strangers' in the world (1 Peter 2.11), with our true citizenship in heaven (Philippians 3.20), caught between the two cultures of the earthly world and the kingdom of God (John 15.18–19).

The *gēr* was quite distinct from the *nokrî*, who is presented as a 'true' foreigner – someone whose loyalties lay in his country of origin, who was a temporary visitor to Israel and who was economically independent. There are various theories about the etymology of the term *nokrî*, none of them positive. It is possibly derived from a Hebrew root meaning to 'recognize' or 'regard': foreigners are those who are 'closely watched'. Other Semitic languages offer meanings including enemy or enmity (Assyrian); evil or change (Arabic); rejection or injury (Sabean). It seems clear that the *nokrî* was viewed with a degree of suspicion and disapproval at best – and perhaps with outright hostility.

The word is frequently used of foreign gods (e.g. Deuteronomy 31.16) which threatened to ensnare the Israelites throughout their history.

In short, in the Israelites' early years, there are few occasions in which the *nokrî*, or anything that is *nokrî*, is presented with anything other than distrust. Between the lines of almost every mention, the *nokrî* is assumed to be abusive, exploitative and untrustworthy (even if the reality of individual cases does not match this, as with Ruth). This explains the differences in how they are treated, compared to the *'ezrāh* and *gēr*. For example, the *only* circumstances in which interest could ever be charged was when an Israelite lent money to a *nokrî* (Deuteronomy 23.19–20).[12]

Integration

Gērîm were invited to integrate fully with Israelite society – often by attaching themselves to a household as a long-term labourer, and by participating in the religious festivals and cultural practices that characterized Israelite life. When they did so, they were treated like native Israelites under the Law: 'A foreigner [*gēr*] residing among you who wants to celebrate the LORD's Passover must have all the males in his household circumcised; then he may take part like one born in the land [*'ezrāh*]. No uncircumcised male may eat it. The same law applies both to the native-born and to the foreigner residing among you' (Exodus 12.48–49). We can assume that *gērîm* were not required to celebrate Passover, but if they wished to then they were welcome – on God's terms, not their own. Fully assimilated or not, the *gērîm* were always to be treated with love and generosity, due to their vulnerability.

This contrasts with the economically independent *nokrî*, who is viewed with more caution. The *nokrî*'s allegiance lies outside of Israel, to a different country and different gods. Their presence is allowed but the threat they represent to Israelite society, culture and religion is recognized – not least in the economic threat they pose, hence the exception to the interest law, which ensures that they pay their way and cannot exploit the Israelites.

Although it is unrealistic to expect one-to-one correspondence, it seems that the biblical *gēr* can most closely be identified with today's asylum seeker or refugee. The Bible's concern for the *gēr* is reflected in the number of times they are mentioned – almost always in the context of vulnerability and need. Many economic migrants may also fall into this category, since they have left their country of origin due to some degree of hardship or limited opportunity, and settled for the long term in the UK – often taking on low-paid jobs that native Britons are unwilling to do.

The *nokrî* is associated with those whose visit is temporary and whose allegiance ultimately lies elsewhere. The foreign student would generally fall into this category, along with some wealthier economic migrants whose relationship with the country could be viewed as short-term and even exploitative. To these we might plausibly add multinational companies which operate in the UK but are domiciled elsewhere or have arrangements in place to avoid paying tax here. Additionally, some British-born high net-worth individuals actually choose to be domiciled elsewhere so that they can avoid paying taxes here; they have essentially taken on *nokrî* status voluntarily. The obligation to pay their way for those who are able, and for the Israelites to provide work, support and community for those who are vulnerable and dependent on them, is a simple yet profound guiding principle.

Broadening horizons

But this is not the beginning and end of the Bible's treatment of immigrants. The early years of the Israelites' existence reflect the circumstances following the exile: their arrival in the promised land and their difficulties in establishing themselves and remaining distinct from Canaanite custom and religion. With the rise of the monarchy and Israelite state, and later during the exile in Babylon, the Jews showed a greater openness to welcoming the sympathetic *nokrî*, though they continued to recognize the threat that pagan religion posed to their national and religious identity. Solomon's prayer of dedication for the new Temple entertains the possibility of the *nokrî* who comes to Israel from 'a distant land' because he has heard of the Lord (1 Kings 8.41–43). Isaiah 56.1–8 likewise entertains the possibility of the foreign convert who is numbered among God's people. This passage discusses exiles and refers to a time when Israel had been forced to look beyond its own borders and to broaden its perspectives.

The qualified invitation to foreigners was grounded in the Israelites' vision for their society: an attractive community that would act as a 'light to the nations' (e.g. Isaiah 49.6). Anyone who was willing to follow the Lord and be a part of that community was welcomed. Otherwise, the default approach was caution. Time and again throughout their history the Israelites had found that foreign religion posed a serious threat.

The Israelites' vision encompassed not only their faith but the kind of society that was supposed to result from it.[13] We can no longer offer a religious vision; the UK in the twenty-first century cannot be characterized as a 'Christian' nation. The failure of multiculturalism left a vacuum, with no strong narratives to take its place. Until we are able to articulate what we stand for as a country, beyond narrow and reductionist clichés about economic growth, we have no other coherent vision to offer those who migrate here, and no clear way to assess the motives of those who do come to the country.

The bottom line

We are, as a nation, confused and misinformed about immigration. What accurate information we do have is subject to spin and exaggeration by certain sections of the media which play on the public's concerns and distort the real picture. The same dynamics risk driving immigration policy. Politicians are too often a part of this collusion and pander to unfounded fears, rather than seek to address them.

We categorize immigrants and restrict their entry and stay based on where they come from (EU, non-EU) and why (study, work, joining a family member, asylum, irregular immigration). The Bible is more interested in the intangible boundaries around Israelite society and religion, not its national borders. Articulating a positive and attractive vision of British society has to be a first step in formulating a credible immigration policy.

Immigrants were typically viewed as vulnerable and dependent (*gēr*) or economically independent (*nokrî*). All were invited to integrate with Israelite society fully, including participating in its religion and festivals, and were treated equally under the Law when they did so. However, the realities were that the *nokrî*'s allegiances generally lay elsewhere. This meant that measures (including economic) had to be taken to protect the Israelites from exploitation by immigrants who had little interest in the welfare of the community.

Points for action
- In what ways has immigration personally benefited you, or otherwise?
- Do your personal experiences fit with the national media and political narrative(s) about immigration?
- How do or will you engage with the issue of immigration beyond the election?

The environment

'Vote blue, go green.' In 2006 David Cameron made the environment a major plank of the Conservatives' local election campaign. The aspiration, that the Conservatives would be recognized as the best party to lead the UK's 'green revolution', was repeated in the 2008 local elections, and again in 2010 in their manifesto for the 2010 General Election.

Since then, the environment has slipped as a concern for voters and politicians alike. Despite being a mixture of blue and yellow, the coalition has failed to realize their promise to be the 'greenest government ever'.[14] As the depth of the recession and the slow and faltering nature of the recovery became painfully clear, key election pledges were quietly left behind: green policies are expensive to implement, and their cost to the nation's businesses threatened the 'green shoots' of economic growth.

This competition with economic recovery has firmly shoved green issues off the centre stage. Although the main parties pay lip-service to the environment, there is no doubt about which is more important. Environmental subsidies have been reduced under the coalition (such as the admittedly over-generous solar feed-in tariff), and the Green Deal, which offers loans for energy-saving home improvements, has been criticized for a number of reasons – not least because the interest rates are significantly higher than other commercially available loans. In 2013, above-inflation price hikes by the big energy companies raised questions about why gas and electricity were so expensive. High green levies were pinpointed as one of the problems (wholesale prices and the cost of transmission are other major components, as well as the companies' profit margins). Reducing green levies even became a political football. David Cameron argued that Labour had introduced them when last in power; Ed Miliband countered that more than half of the cost had been added under the coalition. (Nick Clegg vowed that the Lib Dems would keep green taxes.) Polls showed that the vast majority of the public were against green levies on their energy bills.

In September 2013 a broad alliance of environmental charities criticized all the major parties for their record on green issues. The Conservatives were guilty of 'framing environmental policy as an obstacle to growth', while Labour had given 'no sense that the environment is at the heart' of their policies. But their fiercest attack was reserved for the Lib Dems, for presenting themselves as the party that cared for the environment while failing to live up to their promises. 'Our review shows why the Liberal Democrats are fast losing their image as a "green"

political party. Their failure to stop the chancellor from undermining efforts to cut carbon pollution, and their support for
fracking for more fossil fuels in the English countryside will
have left many of their voters feeling betrayed.'[15]

Among the smaller parties, the Greens obviously represent
a radically different voice on the environment, but they are a
limited political force and it remains to be seen if they will win
any seats in the election. At the other end of both the political
and environmental spectrums, UKIP are openly sceptical about
man-made climate change and vocally oppose investment in
new wind farms and other sources of renewable energy.

Framing the problem biblically

None of the mainstream political parties takes caring for the
environment seriously – and neither, it has to be said, do many
Christians. One strand of Christian culture puts great emphasis on caring for the environment, on the grounds that God
entrusted the world to our care. But another strand more or less
ignores environmental issues, seeing the current created order
as temporary. As the American pastor Mark Driscoll once con-
troversially remarked, 'I know who made the environment and
he's coming back and going to burn it all up. So yes, I drive an
SUV.'[16]

This highlights a major problem: that the subject is typically
characterized by a fixation on climate change and carbon emissions. One result of this is that it enables some people to sidestep the debate entirely, simply by denying either that climate
change is a real phenomenon, or that humans are responsible
for it. But climate change is only one element of caring for
the environment. There are many 'interrelated issues that have
significant implications for our planet. These include lack of
clean drinking water, erosion and degradation of fertile agricul-
tural land, increased risk of flooding as sea levels rise, irrevers-
ible destruction of wildlife habitats, increase in toxic waste and
pollution.'[17]

More subtly damaging than this black/white approach to the environment are the terms we use to understand the problems, and therefore the nature of the solutions we find. A glance at the Conservatives' 2010 manifesto is revealing. It includes an increase in green taxes, the introduction of a carbon floor price, a ban on new coal-fired plants and incentives for recycling. These are economic and political solutions. In fairness, such policy options are the way that government generally has to operate. But this is the language that pervades all of our discussion about the environment: miles per gallon of fuel, parts per million of CO_2, millimetres of sea level, dollars per barrel of oil, degrees centigrade per century, pence increase of fuel tax, kilowatt hours . . .

These are 'somebody else's problem' – matters for scientists to grapple with, or for politicians in Whitehall to negotiate. They are not something that the majority of voters can or need concern themselves with. They do not mention our preference for driving alone rather than commuting by public transport, our frequent foreign holidays, our reliance on tumble dryers and other appliances, our insatiable demand for consumer electronics, our love of central heating, our wasted food, even our full kettles and long showers. They are technological, economic and political solutions, rather than behavioural and relational ones that individuals can personally engage with and be challenged by.

The Bible views things quite differently. It sees environmental problems as symptoms, with relational problems as their underlying cause. Our attitudes towards each other and to God are the root of unsustainable habits. Ultimately, sustainability and the environment aren't matters of science, economics or politics: they are matters of justice.

Creation mandate

There are two opposing mistakes it is easy to make about the environment. The first is assuming that it is unimportant, because it is part of the temporary order that God will one day replace. The Corinthians made the same mistake when they claimed that it didn't matter what they did with their physical, earthly bodies, since the spiritual realm was the only thing that concerned God. Paul urgently had to correct this heresy (1 Corinthians 6.12–20). The second mistake is to idolize creation, elevating it to a status where it competes with God for our loyalty. We are to worship the Creator, not his creation.

God created us, and he created the world as the only physical context for us to exist within. The opening chapters of Genesis include two important passages relating to humans' care for the environment. In Genesis 1.28 God commands humankind to 'fill the earth and subdue it'. But this exercise of dominion over creation cannot imply casual violence towards it, not least because it comes in the context of the preceding verse: 'So God created man in his own image, in the image of God he created him; male and female he created them.' It's also worth noting that filling the earth and subduing it was not intended to be a short-term task. It would take many generations and was an ongoing project. So stewardship of creation is necessarily inter-generational – we need to be looking ahead to the effects on our children and grandchildren of different environmental policies.

The Hebrew word 'image' in Genesis 1.27 is *ṣelem*, which elsewhere in the Bible is used of the graven and cast idols worshipped by neighbouring cultures (e.g. Amos 5.26). These, of course, were supposed to represent pagan gods. The Israelites were forbidden from creating idols: this was one of the distinctive features of Israelite religion. This verse clearly does not refer to our physical similarities, but to our characters. Humans themselves are God's representatives on earth, and as such we are to treat the rest of creation (including each other) in the same way that he does.

The second passage is Genesis 2.15: 'The LORD God took the man and put him in the Garden of Eden to work it and take care of it.' This further qualifies the command to 'subdue' the earth in Genesis 1.28. The purpose is not to destroy it or beat it into submission. It is to tend the garden as a steward.

The Fall brought about not only a rupture in the relationship between God and humans; it also broke the relationship between humans and the environment. 'Cursed is the ground because of you . . .' (Genesis 3.17b). This is not the only time in Scripture that a link is made between sin and harm to the environment. Isaiah 24.4–6 talks of a curse consuming the earth due to the Israelites disobeying God's laws and defiling it. A similar idea is expressed in Jeremiah 12.11–12. Hosea 4.3 makes a connection between sin and environmental catastrophe. 'Because of this the land mourns, and all who live in it waste away; the beasts of the field and the birds of the air and the fish of the sea are dying.'

We can also see a clear link between social injustice and harm to the environment today. Excessive consumption of natural resources goes hand in hand with abuses to human third parties, as well as to the environment. This may happen through very direct means – displacing native populations, polluting their land and water with toxic chemicals, using child labour, and so on. Or it may occur through more indiscriminate mechanisms such as climate change, which disproportionately affects the poorer segments of society. All, however, are a result of a culture that demands more stuff at low prices to satisfy consumer demand and maintain our privileged lifestyles. One difference is that the Bible's link between sin and environmental harm appears as a direct punishment from God, whereas in our modern view it is seen as a logical outcome of our actions: when we treat the environment this way, it is hardly surprising that there are consequences for all of us.

Regardless of how or why the damage occurs, the Bible also sees the redemption of the whole creation as part of God's plan. Paul writes, 'The creation waits in eager expectation for the sons of God to be revealed . . . We know that the whole creation has been groaning as in the pains of childbirth right up to the present time' (Romans 8.19, 22). The book of Revelation looks forward to a time when there will be a 'new heaven and a new earth' (Revelation 21.1). There are two main words used for 'new' in New Testament Greek: *neos* and *kainos*. Although there is some overlap in usage, *neos* broadly refers to things that are chronologically new – that is, they did not exist before. *Kainos* has the meaning of 'new in character' and is often used of the age to come. It is not 'brand new' but 'renewed', restored. In Genesis 1 God called his creation good. His answer to the Fall is not to destroy it and start again from scratch but to redeem it.

Policy areas

A perspective that views environmental issues as an integral part of a broader picture of social justice can help inform how we engage with them as a political issue. At a simple level, we cannot separate out the environment from other key concerns. It cannot be a bolt-on extra that is nice to protect if we can afford it but can be left behind if the cost is too great. How we view the environment and the unsustainable use of resources implicitly affects how we understand economic activity, foreign policy, immigration and other areas of voting.

We need to hold our politicians to account and force them to think beyond the five-year parliaments that characterize so much policy, at the expense of long-term sustainability. Energy policy – currently a major political issue – is one important strand of this. Are they prepared to make a tough stance, or settle for one that pleases voters in the short term but only stores up greater problems further down the line? The same goes for transport – to what extent do they have a vision for a clean transport system, with reliable public transport increasingly taking the place of inefficient private transport?

The bottom line

The Bible cares about the environment because it cares about how people treat God and each other, and how we treat the environment inevitably has third-party effects. Instead of seeing environmental issues as technical, economic or political problems, we need to think of them within the more challenging framework of our behaviour and relationships. Indeed, the Bible doesn't recognize 'the environment' as an impersonal, external entity at all; instead it speaks of animals as 'souls' akin to humans (Ecclesiastes 3.21), of trees and mountains worshipping God (Isaiah 55.12), and of wild beasts, plagues and famines that bring his judgement (Ezekiel 14.21).

Environmental issues are intrinsically connected with issues of justice. Our runaway consumption of natural resources harms not only the planet but the others who share it with us. Recognition of this reality has to underpin environmental policy, rather than merely reducing it to abstract proxies for success like CO_2 emissions.

Points for action

- Politicians make big promises about the environment, but few deliver. Research your MP to find out what decisions he or she has made about major environmental bills in the past.
- Aim to find out how integrated your MP's environmental policy really is – whether he or she has truly thought through the implications or whether the environment is a disconnected afterthought to everything else your MP does. Challenge 'greenwashing' politicians, especially if they have pledged to keep a higher standard.
- What personal habits might you address in the process?

4

Public services

Police, crime and prisons

Levels of crime are at their lowest in over 30 years. In the year to September 2013 alone, crime in England and Wales fell by 10 per cent. The figures from the Office for National Statistics estimate crime levels based on how many people report having been victims of crime, and are therefore independent of the police's own figures (which also fell for the year). The change in violent offences is the most impressive: they have dropped by 60 per cent in the past decade, and the murder rate has almost halved. We are safer now than we have been in a generation.

Despite accusations of interested parties massaging the statistics, or suggestions that people are so resigned to it that they don't report crime any more, there are some offences (like murder) that are beyond manipulation. Hospital admissions for assault and other violent crime have also gone down. So crime really is falling – despite the fact that there are fewer police officers than there were five years ago.

Fear of crime, however, has not kept pace with the falling crime rate. The UK Peace Index[1] found that 17 per cent of Britons think they will be a victim of violent crime, but less than 4 per cent will actually experience violent crime: 'Surveys on perceptions of crime show that people feel crime is falling locally even as they think it is increasing nationally.'

The near-universal explanation for this is that the mass media has a habit of sensationalizing crime, highlighting particularly shocking but isolated and unrepresentative cases from around the country. Good news does not make good news – or, as one *Guardian* journalist put it, 'if it bleeds, it leads'. Fear-based media sells better.

It is probably this disconnect between perceptions of crime and reality that has helped drive another unhelpful tendency: the policing targets culture. 'Processing' offences and recording them is how the public is reassured that the police are doing their job. Put simply, the more incidents recorded, arrests made and convictions secured, the better we know that justice is being done. As in the case of the NHS and education, however, this targets culture can easily give rise to abuses. The police service's own crime figures are treated with an increasing degree of scepticism – the Office for National Statistics removed their stamp of approval from the police's crime data because the UK Statistics Authority questioned their reliability. That the figures are routinely fiddled is an open secret. 'Serving Metropolitan Police officer PC James Patrick told MPs last month that crime figures were manipulated to hit performance targets, adding that this had become "an ingrained part of policing culture".'[2]

The political narrative around crime is all about being 'tough'. New Labour's 1997 manifesto promise of 'tough on crime, tough on the causes of crime' has set the tone ever since. Labour have reiterated this pledge in the last parliament (albeit with qualifications about reducing reoffending) and the Conservatives have also sworn to be 'tough on crime and tough on criminals'.[3] As a result, we lock up many more people than we used to, and proportionally many more than elsewhere in Western Europe. At the time of writing, the prison population for England and Wales is a little over 85,000 – twice the level in the 1980s. Tens of thousands of young people are being tried in front of magistrates when previously they were dealt with outside the formal justice system.

Understanding justice

In the Hebrew Bible, two words repeatedly occur together in the context of justice: ṣedeq (or ṣ^{e}dāqāh) and mišpāṭ, usually translated 'righteousness' and 'justice'. They are closely linked theologically but have different meanings.

Mišpāṭ comes from a root meaning to judge or govern; to act as lawgiver; to decide controversy, condemn or punish.[4] The noun *mišpāṭ* can mean several things, including the act of deciding a case; the seat of judgement; process or litigation before judges; a legal sentence or decision; and the execution of judgement. This is something like our modern understanding of justice: a process that puts right a wrong.

The word *ṣedeq* has a different set of connotations. Related verbs mean to be just, righteous in conduct/character; to be in the right, to have a right cause. In another form they mean to justify, vindicate the cause of, or save. So 'righteousness' in the Bible means what is right, just, normal – whether in speech, government, a legal case, or even the weights and measures described in Deuteronomy 25.15.

In *Generous Justice*, Tim Keller argues that *mišpāṭ* is 'rectifying justice' (referring either to punishment or receiving one's rights) and *ṣᵉdāqāh* is 'primary justice' – the conditions of right relationship that would render rectifying justice unnecessary if widely practised. Together, he says, the words have the rough meaning of 'social justice'.[5] 'Doing justice includes not only the righting of wrongs but generosity and social concern, especially toward the poor and vulnerable.'

Jonathan Burnside has a similar approach, though he looks at it the other way round. People are considered 'righteous' when they have fulfilled the conditions imposed on them by relationships, and proper justice leads to righteousness.

> This concern for right relationships is reflected in the Hebrew term *ṣᵉdāqāh* ('righteousness', although the word itself is not restricted to a concern for right relationships) . . . *Ṣᵉdāqāh* is the goal of *mišpāṭ* (justice), and both 'justice and righteousness' (*mišpāṭ ûṣᵉdāqāh*) are major concerns of the prophets (e.g. Isaiah 56.1 . . .) Israel's righteousness is to be seen in her relationship with God, the nations, and at the level of relationships between individual Israelites.[6]

This is reflected in Jesus' summary of the Law and Prophets in Matthew 22.34–40.

These interpretations broadly agree: justice is the action, righteousness is the state of being that results – and, in turn, leads to justice.

God is the ultimate source of justice. It is part of his character: 'He is the Rock, his works are perfect, and all his ways are just [*mišpāṭ*]. A faithful God who does no wrong, upright [*ṣaddîq*] and just is he' (Deuteronomy 32.4). But there is more to God's character than justice, or even the righteousness that is the goal of justice. Of God's many attributes – justice, love, compassion, truth, holiness – perhaps the most important and all-encompassing of the others is his *ḥesed*: his loving-kindness or covenant love.[7] This becomes apparent in Hosea's metaphor of the undeserved but continued relationship between God and Israel, which includes many other characteristics of God: 'I will betroth you to me for ever; I will betroth you in righteousness and justice, in love [*ḥesed*] and compassion [*raḥᵃmîm*]. I will betroth you in faithfulness [*'ᵉmûnāh*], and you will acknowledge the LORD' (Hosea 2.19–20). This loving-kindness or covenant love (often simply translated as 'mercy') includes a concern for justice and righteousness. As Jonathan Burnside writes, 'because justice is a characteristic of God himself, it is inseparable from God's other characteristics, including his kindness, his love and his righteousness (which encompasses a concern for "right relationships").'[8]

When we read the Bible, and especially the Old Testament, we often assume that 'justice' requires only a transaction. It is a quid pro quo: an eye for an eye (Deuteronomy 19.21). A crime deserves a punishment; only then has justice been done. This is not so far from our own transactional, retributive approach to justice.

But this is a distortion of the biblical view of justice, for several reasons. One is simply that the *lex talionis* – the eye-for-an-eye principle – was intended to limit punishment, not set its appropriate level. It means '*only* an eye for an eye'. It was designed to prevent blood feuds from escalating out of control. Another, more important reason, is that the Old Testament sees justice as relational, not procedural. Rather than being a matter of carrying out a transaction such as a fine or other punishment, the purpose wherever possible was to restore the relationship that the crime had disrupted. This is clear from the idea of restitution in Exodus 21—22. In the New Testament, Jesus reframes the eye-for-an-eye law and teaches that even measured, limited revenge for injury is not the ideal that God desires. Better than exacting equal punishment is to love your enemy (Matthew 5.38–39). The crucifixion was the supreme example of God's forgoing of the *lex talionis* and the ultimate restoration of broken relationships.

A further point is that justice was, wherever possible, based on family and community. Local courts pronounced judgement in disputes, with cases only passed up to a higher, centralized authority when they were too difficult for the local elders (Deuteronomy 17.8–10). The same was true for other legal matters such as property transactions (see Ruth 4). Although there was some provision for social exclusion in serious cases, such as manslaughter (Numbers 35), the ideal was restoration back into the community.

Justice at a distance

This ideal of community-based justice with restoration as its ideal is a far cry from our consumerized view of justice. Instead of getting our hands dirty with the messy realities of relationships with those who have wronged us, we choose the superficially easier way of paying others to carry out justice. We pass responsibility over to the state, resigning control over it in the process. With a few exceptions, such as the restorative justice programmes in which victims and perpetrators meet before sentencing, bringing about justice is someone else's job. We have adopted a black-and-white view of criminal justice. When a person is on the wrong side of the law, we wash our hands of him or her. At best, this leads to an impersonal and dehumanizing approach to justice. This is not what the Bible advocates. In fact, the dignity of the perpetrator was a key principle, as well as the needs of the victim (Deuteronomy 25.1–3). As Nelson Mandela said, 'A country should be judged, not by how it treats its highest citizens, but how it treats its lowest ones.'

The bigger picture

Finally, a look at the backgrounds of those within the prison system suggests that we should have a smarter approach than simply being 'tough' on crime. Over a quarter of prisoners come from a background in care, 70 per cent misuse drugs prior to their time in prison and almost half of the prison population has an addiction to drugs. Most of these inmates will be in prison for crimes connected to their addiction.[9] Anyone with a criminal record is discounted from around half of all job opportunities, and only a third of those leaving prison go into education, training or paid work. The majority have a history of truancy and/or exclusion from school, and nearly a third of prisoners have nowhere to live on their release. A lack of education and rehab in prison means that most prisoners are no better off when they leave than when they went in, and around half will reoffend.

The bottom line

It is those who are already most marginalized in society who are most likely to have contact with the criminal justice system. The Bible expects offenders to take responsibility for their crimes and to make restitution, but that is one half of a two-way contract with the rest of society. Criminal justice must be seen as part of a coherent strategy that addresses wider marginalization: education, welfare, employment, debt, addiction and family breakdown – as well as serving the needs of the law-abiding majority.

Points for action

- Have you been the victim of a crime recently? What was your response – and what might you do differently if it happened again?
- Do your prospective MPs' approaches go beyond 'tough on crime' rhetoric?
- To what extent is crime policy understood as part of a wider strategy of social integration?

Education

'Our top priority was, is and always will be education, education, education.' Tony Blair's education manifesto for Labour's second term in government made it very clear where his aspirations lay. For that parliament alone, Blair promised 10,000 more teachers, 20,000 more classroom assistants, a step-change in standards, and a goal of 50 per cent of young adults progressing to higher education by 2010.[10] The Labour years saw a huge influx of funds into education after underinvestment by the previous government, against the intended Conservative programme of cuts.

Education is one of those public services, like the NHS, that is sacrosanct to the public – and woe betide any government that tries to save money at the expense of our children's future. The last Labour government pumped money into education. The coalition did not have any money to pump, whether or not they were inclined to, and had to promise improvement by other means. They pledged to open up the schools system to competition, giving parents, teachers, religious groups and charities the power to set up new schools.

The flurry of political activity that occurs around education year in, year out, and especially at election time indicates its importance to politicians and the public alike. Voters, not to mention teachers, have grown weary at the constant stream of initiatives and directives aimed at raising standards. On the surface, these have had some apparent effect: GCSE pass rates rose every year since they were introduced in 1986 (prompting concerns of 'grade inflation') until 2012 when they dropped for the first time (prompting concerns that pupils were being graded too harshly).

Accusations of grade inflation and 'teaching to the test' skip over a more important question. They don't state what education is *for*, though they assume that whatever that purpose is can be measured through exam results.

What is education for?

'We will change the system so that all state schools can use the top exams which prepare children for the best jobs.'[11] Michael Gove's pledge in 2008 made it clear that the purpose of education is to access the highest-paying jobs. Like the way we look at so many aspects of public policy, the argument is an economic one. Get education right and our personal and collective finances will benefit.

It is unfair to characterize education policy entirely in these terms. Tony Blair's appeal in 2001 included these words:

> At a good school children gain the basic tools for life and work. But they ought also to learn the joy of life: the exhilaration of music, the excitement of sport, the beauty of art, the magic of science. And they learn the value of life: what it is to be responsible citizens who give something back to their community.

(In fact, a major pressure on schools in recent years has been to compensate for poor parenting, instilling basic values, discipline, and teaching very basic social and practical skills.)

It's equally clear that preparing Britain for tough international competition in standards and results is a major and growing issue for politicians. Michael Gove began that 2008 speech with the words:

Our living standards and quality of life are going to be profoundly affected over the next decade by three forces – first, the rise of Asia; second, the increasing importance of high technology and, third, the growing gap in education standards between the richest and poorest in our society.

If the explicit purpose of education is to gain the best jobs and earn the most money, our schools will promote materialism and individualism. This is hardly surprising, since our culture is a highly individualistic and consumeristic one, and these values will naturally feed into education. This world-view essentially asks the question, 'What's in it for me?' Education is a tool for self-advancement and the individualistic pursuit of success, whether that success is academic or material.

A biblical view of education

Love the LORD your God with all your heart and with all your soul and with all your strength. These commandments that I give you today are to be on your hearts. Impress them on your children. Talk about them when you sit at home and when you walk along the road, when you lie down and when you get up. Tie them as symbols on your hands and bind them on your foreheads. Write them on the door-frames of your houses and on your gates.

These words, from Deuteronomy 6.5–9, reveal a completely different reason for and approach to education.

We cannot directly compare our twenty-first-century system of schooling with the education practices of the early Israelites. With an agrarian rather than high-tech, service-driven economy, there was little need for formal schools – though some may have existed to serve particular professions. The purpose of education was to bring children up to know and keep God's commandments, teaching holiness and preserving Israel's religious and cultural identity. Proverbs calls this 'Wisdom': understanding the right way to live in community with God and neighbour. Proverbs 9.10 reads: 'The fear of the LORD is the beginning of wisdom.' Another verse in the Wisdom literature reads, 'Fear God and keep his commandments, for this is the whole duty of man' (Ecclesiastes 12.13b). Jesus' own development followed this 'curriculum' in Luke 2.52. This emphasis on Wisdom, character and community is very different from our modern preoccupation with individual advancement.

The way that education was carried out was different, too – partly as a result of the different vision for society that underpinned it, and partly, of course, because of the different cultural setting. The most important strand of education happened at home, with children taught God's laws by parents and the extended family. Beyond that, the Levites had an educational role. They essentially acted as public servants, with remits in health, justice, finance, education and other areas of life. Part of this involved teaching those who came to them for one reason or another to empower them, so that next time they would be able to address the issue themselves. This is the implication of Deuteronomy 17.8–11. It was also the Levites' task periodically to teach the whole of Israel the Law (Deuteronomy 31.10–13). The regular Sabbaths and festivals throughout the year served as further reminders of Israelite history, identity and practice. In the New Testament, the Pharisees took on this role in the synagogues, along with other itinerant teachers (including Jesus and Paul).

At the very least, then, parents were expected to instruct their children on a day-to-day basis, but the Levites were there as a (presumably formally educated) body of teachers who acted as a kind of quality control to ensure that the 'curriculum' was accurately passed down from generation to generation. This is entirely in keeping with the ethos of Israelite political organisation, in which responsibility was characteristically given first to the smallest and most local elements, with higher and more centralised authorities only stepping in where necessary as a kind of failsafe.[12]

Education in the Bible was a distributed, cross-cutting activity that took place in every area and at every stage of life. Its purpose was not to create a handful of specialists in different professions; it was to ensure that everybody had access to the Law and the information they needed to participate in every aspect of their corporate lives. This is what is meant by the words, 'you will be for me a kingdom of priests and a holy nation' in Exodus 19.6. (Former Chief Rabbi Jonathan Sacks has argued that this verse also refers to an ideal of universal literacy, since in Egyptian and other Ancient Near Eastern cultures, reading and writing were the preserve of an elite priesthood. The Hebrew alphabet, which was a simple set of 22 letters rather than the hundreds or even thousands of syllables or hieroglyphs of other neighbouring countries, made this theoretically possible.[13]) The foundational stage of this lifelong education happened at home.

Changing how we think about education

It is worth remembering that state education grew out of church initiatives in the nineteenth century. Today, a significant proportion of schools in the UK are church schools, though the ethos of these can be very different, from explicitly Christian to communicating broad values derived from the Christian tradition. These schools typically 'perform' better than average, meaning that pupils gain a greater proportion of passes in key exams – leading to some curious comments from policymakers about using the winning formula employed by faith schools, but omitting the religious aspects!

The world-view of education is never neutral. It always fosters a vision of society. But the debate over faith schools – whether they should be allowed to proliferate, whether they should be able to select pupils by their (parents') faith – is only one aspect of education policy relevant to Christians. The shift we would like to see in education is from an individualistic, economically driven approach to one that sees education as a means of benefiting society as a whole. These two visions are broadly reflected in two school mottos from the same local area. One states, 'We are proud of who we are'; the other that they are committed to 'Achieving together'. It is no coincidence that the latter is a faith school.

Educationalist Rob Loe writes of how our economic focus has turned education into an 'extension of capitalism', valuing technical and practical knowledge at the expense of the relational.

> Other languages akin to our own even demarcate this distinction; take German for example where '*wissen*' (know that), '*können*' (know how) are quite separate entities of knowing. But linking knowledge to economic goals prevents a third kind of relational knowing: this knowledge of the 'personal' enables individuals to connect far more meaningfully to the world around them and serve it.[14]

Shifting the emphasis of education away from the self and towards the benefit of society as a whole involves changing the way we think about many aspects of it. For a start, we need to end the conflation of 'schooling' with education. This leads to a situation in which education is effectively outsourced to schools, with little or no engagement required at home. Yet we know (both from common-sense observation and research studies) that relationships in the home are the biggest factor for achievement at school: parents taking an interest in their children's education, reading with them, helping them with their homework and providing support. Improving relationships of all kinds in the schools system raises the engagement and attainment of pupils, but the parent–child relationship is the most critical, and, if non-existent or weak for one reason or another, improving the teacher–pupil relationship brings the next biggest benefit. Finally, improving pupil–pupil relationships makes a significant difference.

The way we think about education as a private investment for the benefit of the individual leads to other problems. This 'consumption' of education is most explicit in the context of university tuition fees. Labour's aspiration to see 50 per cent of school leavers going on to university has had the side effect of driving up personal debt. There is now far more competition for the same jobs, and inevitably many graduates are disappointed with the employment they can access. Prizing academic learning (the 'knowing that') so far above practical and particularly relational skills gives with one hand while taking away with the other. Many students will start their working lives £50,000 in debt and may never pay off the money they owe – with long-term implications for them and for taxpayers.

The bottom line

Education has become 'an extension of capitalism': a commodity that we buy as an investment. Its world-view typically focuses on the benefits to the consumer, reinforcing an individualistic mindset. Quite aside from ignoring the networks of relationships of which we are all a part and on which we all rely, this brings problems of its own, including grade inflation, teaching to the test, falling standards, indebtedness and difficulty in securing appropriate employment. An aspiration that everyone should be able to access the best-paying jobs – the 'all must have prizes' mentality – clearly has fundamental problems.

The Bible sees education as far better integrated into our wider relationships – most importantly at home, but throughout the community and life in general. Facilitating this through flexible working practices and family-friendly policy is key to improving education, both in its narrowest academic sense and in its broadest sense of preparing people for full and meaningful participation in every area of life.

Points for action

• If education starts at home, how do you make the time to ensure this?

• In what ways can you become more involved at school – through PTAs, as a school governor, or simply through greater participation as a parent in school life and at the school gate?

• Which party looks beyond the school and has a meaningful idea of what 'education' really entails – and how to improve it?

The NHS

The National Health Service is the closest thing the English have to a religion, with those who practise in it regarding themselves as a priesthood. This made it quite extraordinarily difficult to reform. For a bunch of laymen, who called themselves the Government, to presume to tell the priesthood that they must change their ways in any respect whatever, was clearly intolerable. And faced with a dispute between their priests and ministers, the public would have no hesitation in taking the part of the priesthood.[15]

So wrote former Chancellor Nigel Lawson, and indeed the NHS has been a poisoned chalice for politicians for years. The British public are in thrall to the idea of universal healthcare, free at the point of access. Anyone who tinkers with it risks their wrath. Unfortunately, leaving it alone is not an option. The needs of an ageing population mean that the NHS has had to do more and more in recent years – and the state of the nation's finances means that it has had less and less with which to do it.

Over the last 20 years, spending on the NHS has leapt from £40.5 billion in 1995 to a projected £132.6 billion in 2015, almost tripling per head. Most of that surge occurred in the

Labour years. Since the money ran out and the austerity programme has taken effect, the coalition have pledged to ringfence NHS spending, despite other departments suffering heavy cuts.

What is health?

Ask a group of people what they think 'health' is and you will probably receive several different answers. At its most basic level it is the absence of illness or injury. This negative definition simply acknowledges that healthy people don't need to visit a doctor or hospital – that they are functioning adequately.

The World Health Organization states, 'Health is a state of complete physical, mental and social well-being and not merely the absence of disease or infirmity.' Dissatisfied with this definition, which was first given in 1948, contributors to the *British Medical Journal* proposed 'a new definition of health as "the ability to adapt and self manage" in the face of social, physical, and emotional challenges'.[16] This implies that health is about resilience, rather than an idealized state of well-being.

Over the course of the last parliament our national narratives about health have changed, too. The recent inquiry into the Stafford hospital scandal, in which hundreds of patients died unnecessarily between 2005 and 2008 due to inadequate care and poor management, was probably the most high-profile example of NHS failings. On a different note, there is gradual recognition that the ageing population will bring with it the need for vastly increased healthcare spending. The looming 'dementia crisis' has gained attention in recent years; approaching a million people in the UK suffer from dementia, with age being the single biggest risk factor. The risk is one in 14 for a 65-year-old, but one in six for an 80-year-old. Caring for someone with dementia costs around £28,000 annually. At present most of this is borne by carers, but as the number of patients increases the NHS will be expected to fund more. Another dynamic that has shifted narratives about healthcare is better understanding of mental health conditions, their interaction with behavioural and physical conditions, and the way they affect people's ability to engage with society and employment.

Health suddenly seems a lot more complicated than it used to be, but our expectations of the NHS are higher than ever. Those expectations drive public policy, but they also drive the approach of healthcare practitioners and managers to their work. The targets culture has given rise to all kinds of abuses, such as 'patient stacking': the practice of emergency patients being left in ambulances, so that trusts could meet their target of treating every patient within four hours of entering the hospital. On the public's side, we still want our universal health-care, free at the point of access, and that means expensive drugs to treat conditions we previously wouldn't have lived long enough to experience. What should the NHS pay for? The ongoing debate over whether those suffering from conditions related to smoking, obesity and alcohol should contribute to the cost of their treatment illustrates the tension between the desire to provide a universal service and the problems in meeting the costs of that.

The Bible and healthcare

Neither early Israel nor the early Church enjoyed a comprehensive system of healthcare like the NHS, but we can still apply the principles we see in the Bible. The Levites took on different roles as public servants, including treating medical conditions and educating the public about healthcare. Some of the Bible's laws apparently supported practices that benefited health and limited the spread of disease, though the degree to which holiness, rather than health, was the priority is not clear. There was, however, some emphasis on prevention as well as cure.

Concern for human well-being lies at the heart of God's desire for his creation. The idea of *imago Dei* – that we are created in God's image – underpins belief in the dignity of humankind and equal worth, regardless of income or status. This, and Jesus' statement in Matthew 25.40, 'whatever you did for one of the least of these brothers of mine, you did for me', suggests that our ideal of universal healthcare is a biblically sound one.

However, there are two sides to this. Universal healthcare is just that: universal. The problem is that we tend to see this in terms of our own rights to receive treatment when we need it. We don't look at it from the other side of the equation: that *my* use of the NHS necessarily affects all of its other users, and the degree to which it truly can remain universal.

In the Bible, personal responsibility and corporate responsibility are not compartmentalized. One implication of Jesus' summary of the Law and the Prophets in Matthew 22 is that we are accountable both to God and to other people. There is no example of Jesus refusing to heal someone, but Jesus did recognize that illness could occur through a person's own sin, someone else's, or for different reasons entirely (John 5.14; 9.1–3). If we accept the benefits of universal healthcare, there is also a challenge for us to take greater responsibility – both for our own health, and for the consequences of our actions on the health and access to healthcare for others. We need to regain a sense of the corporate, that my 'personal' decisions and lifestyle have impacts on others.

Alongside that, the Bible's view of health is far more meaningful and holistic than the narrow biomedical one we often settle for today. Instead of a simple absence of infirmity, or even resilience, the Hebrew Bible talks about *shalom*: a state of completeness or general well-being, reflected in all areas of life – the medical, but also the financial/economic, relational and spiritual. There is far more to health than lack of disease. The World Health Organization's apparently impossible definition of 'complete physical, mental and social well-being', while omitting any spiritual element, is closer than most to this ideal.

In the Bible, health is not just important because being unhealthy is unpleasant for the individual. Long life and good health allow you to participate in society and engage in relationships. Crucially, from a modern perspective, health enables you *to fulfil your relational obligations* – to look after those who need your care and to provide for your dependents. Health is not just about the individual: it is intimately connected to the ability of the individual to support others and play a part in family and society.

Consumer health

If consumerism is our culture's guiding ideology, then we have applied it to health as much as we have to the purchase of clothing, coffee and electronics. Consumerism has 'productized' health, turning it from a lifelong activity in which we necessarily participate into a product that can be bought and consumed. One of the most overt examples of this is the mass provision of statins. Statins are a class of drugs that lower cholesterol, protecting against heart attacks and strokes, and have been available to around 7 million people who were judged to have a 20 per cent chance of developing cardiovascular disease over the next ten years. This provision was based on risk factors including age, sex, weight and smoking habits. They have been estimated to save around 7,000 deaths a year, for 10 pence per patient per day. In February 2014, NICE (National Institute for Health and Care Excellence) recommended that they should be made even more widely available, and that anyone with a 10 per cent risk over the next ten years should take them.

Because they save so many lives every year, along with preventing tens of thousands of serious but non-fatal attacks, the cost–benefit analysis for statins is overwhelmingly clear. But the reality remains that these drugs are effectively used to treat lifestyle conditions and social issues, not just medical ones. We don't look after ourselves, then we purchase a cheap fix. That speaks volumes about our assumptions about healthcare.

One of the most popular policies put forward to fix our overloaded healthcare system is a return to 'old-fashioned nursing' that gives real attention to patients' needs (including food and basic hygiene, as well as emotional needs), rather than merely viewing them as a set of symptoms to be fixed. As Health Secretary Jeremy Hunt promised, 'we are launching a new vision for nursing, which will put compassion and the patient at the heart of what nurses do'.[17]

This is, of course, necessary – in fact it seems so obvious to put 'the patient at the heart of what nurses do' that it should not even *need* reiterating. But even this doesn't recognize that overloaded staff and poor care are a result of the vast increase in numbers of patients and a targets culture that confuses being *seen* to care with providing quality care itself.

Tackling this problem at its source is about more than changing medical practices and accountability. Behavioural and social changes will be far more important than medical technology. The reality is that medical professionals play (as they should) a comparatively small part in maintaining our health. As Ian McColl, former Professor of Surgery at Guy's and St Thomas' hospital in London, wrote, 'It often comes as a surprise for some medical students that the health of a nation is more dependent on public health and social issues than the clinical activities of doctors. The reduction in tuberculosis over [the twentieth] century in this country has much more to do with nutrition and housing than medicines.'[18]

Whereas the greatest threats were once diseases like tuberculosis and cholera, and their solutions better nutrition, sanitation and housing, the killers are now cancer, heart disease and diabetes. Obesity, poor diet, alcohol abuse, smoking and inactivity form a cluster of major risk factors for these. In fact, for the five most serious conditions – heart disease, stroke, cancer, lung disease and liver disease – the Department of Health estimates that a fifth of the more than 150,000 deaths a year among those under 75 in England could be completely avoided.[19]

The bottom line

The biggest challenges facing the NHS are not medical. They are cultural and behavioural. Our mindset of personal freedom undermines the ability of the NHS to do its job by overloading it, both with excessive and avoidable cases and excessive expectations. Addressing this will mean taking greater responsibility for our health and that of others, reflecting the fact that good health has implications for our ability to interact with other people and support them, as well as for our own subjective well-being.

For politicians, this will mean awkward conversations about personal lifestyle and challenging the world-view that other people should be responsible for our health because we are unwilling to take the burden on ourselves. Few politicians have the appetite for that kind of controversy, but without radical changes in the way we treat ourselves and, by extension, the NHS, we are headed for a far greater squeeze on resources.

Points for action

- Do you view your health in terms of its impact on your own life, or the degree to which it allows you to engage with others and fulfil your obligations to those who need you?
- Is your MP prepared to address uncomfortable realities of unhealthy lifestyle as well as medical provision?
- What are the different parties' approaches to the targets culture? Do they see beyond this to meaningful care?

5

The relational manifesto

Bridging the gap

Votewise 2015 aims to give Christians a biblical framework for understanding the issues that affect voters, but it stops short of recommending specific policies. It also does not advocate the formation or promotion of an explicitly Christian political party or manifesto.

Although this might sound like an obvious step, it raises several issues. One is simply the pragmatic concern that there are comparatively few Christians to field as candidates; it is easier to work within the existing system. Second, political parties deal primarily in policies. Although their values and principles should set their agenda, it is their policies that they present to voters. There may be many different ways that a principle could be expressed in policy. If people disagree with the policies of a Christian party, as they reasonably might, there is an association between those policies and the Christian faith that may put people off Christianity itself.

This chapter aims to bridge the gap between exploring biblical principles for society and articulating specific policies based on that Judaeo-Christian world-view. It suggests a framework for putting these principles into practice in a secular society that does not share the Christian faith, plus a brief 'manifesto' of sample policies. This means using ideas and language that resonate with non-Christian as well as Christian politicians and voters, and that are mainstream enough to have broad appeal.[1]

Diagnosing symptoms and causes

Dissatisfaction with the political process has never been greater. Leadership in all spheres appears to have failed: in politics and the public sector, but also in finance and business. Politicians are viewed as corrupt or out of touch; bankers as dishonest and irresponsible; energy company chiefs as greedy and manipulative. The financial crisis, LIBOR scandal, pensions shortfalls, hospital staffing issues, energy prices, immigration, employment and benefits – question marks over all of these have convinced the electorate that no one can be trusted to do a good job. So far the web of problems has resisted efforts to fix it. Neither the free market nor public ownership has worked. Tougher regulation has not stopped the abuses it was designed to prevent.

An effective solution requires accurate diagnosis. What all of these problems have in common is not so much a failure of the economic system or of regulatory frameworks. It is a failure of relationships. Lehman Brothers, for example, was characterized by dysfunctional relationships between the bank and stakeholders, and within the company at its highest levels. Details about the bank's performance and vulnerabilities were hidden for many years from the public, rating agencies, government regulators, and even Lehman's own board of directors.[3] Lehman's financial problems could have been addressed, if it weren't for its relational difficulties.

Context informs content

The decisions we make in any given circumstances will depend on the way that we approach an issue. Whatever those decisions are, the day-to-day choices we make or the really big decisions of life, like getting married, buying a house, or choice of career, the framework within which we understand the issues informs our thought processes. Put another way, each decision is informed by the context within which we place the issue.

Take buying a house. Is our context financial? If so, we will choose a place that has a high probability of increasing in value or returning a good rental yield. Is it environmental? In that case we will probably opt for a smaller, well-insulated, energy-efficient building. Or is it relational? Then we will want to assess its location in terms of its proximity to friends, relatives, work and other key relationships, and the opportunities the space gives us to entertain and accommodate guests.

Our consumer-focused culture is not good at assigning meaningful context. All too often the criteria according to which the context is assigned are narrowly financial. This is how we understand economic activity and growth: our standard metric for success is GDP. However, material wealth is a poor indicator of true well-being.[3] As surveys and studies repeatedly show, it is our relationships with those closest to us that we believe makes life worth living. Neither does the amount of money a business generates reflect how just or worthwhile it is. An environmental disaster like an oil spill can raise GDP due to the cost of clean-up. Financial return is not the same as true economic value.

The relational manifesto

Dissatisfaction wins and loses elections. It is rarely the brilliance of one or other party's ideas that convince the electorate to switch their support: it is their frustration with the status quo and the hope that the opposition will be able to do a better job. Voters do not choose the best party. They choose the least worst one.

A common complaint is that all the main parties now look similar, with less and less to distinguish them. One reason for this is that all the parties share the same underlying framework of individualism that is assumed essential but is both driven by and results in an increasingly unworkable situation:

1 **Unsustainable demand for public services.** This stems from the rights culture and the breakdown of the extended family, meaning that more people than ever want services that would previously have been provided by others. This is combined with unsustainable levels of debt and the loss of personal freedom. The results are high levels of taxation and public discontent.

2   **A dysfunctional financial sector** characterized by reward without responsibility and investment without involvement. The relational distance in the corporate world promotes greed and corruption and leads to:

- owners of capital who become absentee landlords
- income disparities and pensions raided by financial intermediaries
- long working hours
- poor business performance and underemployment
- withdrawal of licence to operate and political intervention.

3   **A consumer culture** based on instant self-gratification through choice and easy credit. This leads to the debt-enslavement of the population and disempowerment of the workforce, since fewer people can afford to 'rock the boat'.

Since the financial crisis there has been much talk of reforming capitalism, yet the work carried out to date has been little more than tinkering around the edges. But, as stated in Chapter 1, business as usual is not an option.

> If Capitalism is not radically reformed, what is the alternative? Family and community solidarity will become increasingly dysfunctional, leading to high levels of unemployment, unsustainable demands on schools, hospitals and social services, and an increasingly angry, disillusioned and frustrated electorate. The door will be open for authoritarian politicians of the Left or Right, with an agenda of savage repression to maintain social order. Rather than wait for these sinister alternatives to emerge, Christians need to read the signs of the times.[4]

One question is where to intervene. Governments can only achieve limited goals and must prioritize just a few things. There is also the question of *how* to intervene. Rather than banning certain practices or trying to force people to act a particular way, a more effective and palatable solution is arguably to incentivize change, giving people the motivation, opportunity and support to act in a way that they likely would anyway, if they were able.[5]

Thinking relationally

People used to think that the sun went round the earth. In the sixteenth century, the astronomer Nicolaus Copernicus suggested that in fact the earth goes round the sun, because this made better sense of the evidence he observed. The term 'Copernican revolution' is now used to mean any paradigm shift or fundamental change in the way we understand something.

Relational thinking seeks to bring about a Copernican revolution in public life, placing relationships of all kinds at the centre of the decisions we make, rather than treating them as collateral damage or as a means to an end. This is rooted in the Judaeo-Christian teaching of the Bible.

Thinking relationally does *not* mean choosing relationships rather than money, or pursuing social goals over economic growth. We are *always* doing relationships in one way or another – it's just that we're often doing them badly. Public policy must recognize this rather than ignoring relational consequences (which often come with financial costs, too). 'Triple testing' assesses the impact of a policy in three different spheres: the economic, the environmental and the relational. While the first two are commonly recognized, the third is less often taken into account. We need to ask whether the different parties' policies reflect, foster and maintain healthy relationships, or all but ignore them. Does government empower us to protect and engage in the relationships that matter the most?

Relational policies

The suggested policies below are radical – meaning that they are far-reaching, but also in the original sense of going back to the root of the problem. Some of them will be controversial, but this is partly because it is preferable to give more extreme versions that highlight the problems and potential solutions and show the ultimate intention than watered-down ones that make compromises. Few cost much up front.

1 **Bring about a shift from individual rights to relational rights and responsibilities.** Relational public policy recognizes that we all exist within a complex network of relationships, and every decision we make involves third parties, intentionally or otherwise. An exclusive focus on the individual ignores this, often to the detriment of those third parties.

2 **Create time for people to meet their obligations outside the workplace.** Long working hours mean that people are often unable to care to the extent they would like for their children, dependent elderly people and others who are vulnerable. Instead, these functions have been taken over by the state – disempowering the family in the process.

   • Promote a shared day off work per week (Sunday). Reduce non-essential services so that others are not forced to work and can spend time with friends and family.
   • Introduce a maximum 48-hour working week. Germany, one of the most prosperous nations in Europe, has a 40-hour maximum.

3 **Reduce debt.** Debt is a form of modern-day slavery, with many poorer families permanently trapped in poverty by unpayable debts. High student debts, which normalize borrowing for a person's lifetime, might be avoided by taxing

graduates' earnings at a higher rate. We also need to incentivize the transfer of equity between generations.

4 **Empower families and communities to deliver health,
   welfare and education**. Most savings and insurance decisions are made at the individual level, but family 'savings syn-
   dicates' would enable extended families to make collective
   and strategic, long-term investments for their futures.[6] Tax
   allowances would permit them to use these to buy insurance
   at a discount, and to pool their savings to invest in housing
   and for education and elderly care.

5 **Increase business responsibility**. Revise the corporate
   governance code to include relational reporting, alongside
   financial and environmental factors. Following the King III
   Report in South Africa, businesses have to make public the
   quality of their stakeholder relationships. The same should be
   true in the UK. We also recommend reducing the blanket
   nature of limited liability, which means that shareholders bear
   no responsibility for what is done with their money and in
   their financial interests.

6 **Localize welfare and healthcare decisions**. Shifting spending decisions to local committees would mean that welfare
   and healthcare resources were allocated by those who understand them best, rather than a remote centralized bureaucracy.
   The role of central or regional government would only be to
   set minimum national standards and to intervene where individuals fall through the safety net for one reason or another.

7 **Break up the banks**. The big banks currently rely on the
   international money markets for funding and treat small and
   medium enterprises as a sideshow. They also have immense
   lobbying power that influences Westminster. Breaking up
   the Big Four (RBS, Lloyds, Barclays, HSBC) into nine or

ten regional banks would address this, encouraging them to engage with their local communities, take fewer risks and provide a useful service. The move would likely cost several billion pounds per bank and would be self-financed.

6

Why vote for . . . ?

The previous edition of *Votewise* included short statements by three MPs – essentially party 'pitches', exploring why Christians might be prompted to vote for each of the main parties. This edition expands the number of contributors to five, since the Green Party now has a seat and UKIP has overtaken the Lib Dems as the third largest party by share of the projected vote, albeit without having any MPs to date. It also takes a more personal look at Christianity and politics, asking the contributors about the role their faith has played in their careers and choice of party.

Why I am a Conservative

Elizabeth Berridge

Elizabeth Berridge studied law and practised as a barrister before entering politics, standing as an MP for Stockport in the 2005 General Election. She was appointed Executive Director of the Conservative Christian Fellowship the following year. In 2011 she was made a life peer as Baroness Berridge of the Vale of Catmose in the County of Rutland, the youngest female member of the House of Lords.

I joined the Conservative Party on a point of political principle, though I never thought I would. I grew up near Corby, which was decimated in the 1980s by the closure of the steel works, and I also rejected Conservatism during my teenage years as I thought it was synonymous with individualism. The latter I was always suspicious of, even before I became a Christian, as I had always thought that the community, charity and the family were vital institutions. I also saw the damage that the Eastern European authoritarian states had done to people's freedom of conscience, as well as to those civil society institutions.

My instincts were only confirmed when I looked at the Old Testament and saw how power was divided up between institutions such as the Prophets, Priests and Kings. The passage in Deuteronomy 17 which outlines the roles of judges at different levels of society was also persuasive. Then, of course, there was the classic passage in the New Testament of 'giving to Caesar what is Caesar's and to God what is God's', which has various layers of meaning including that there is a dominion for the state and a dominion for the Church. By this time I knew what I

believed, but I did not know that this carried the label 'conservatism' until I was at Bar School. At one of the mandatory dining
nights I happened to sit next to someone who was already a
member of the Conservative Party, and he wisely just asked me
what I believed. When I outlined that essentially I believed in
a small state and strong communities and civic institutions, he
then informed me I was a 'Wet Tory', which came as quite a
shock. After this chance encounter, the more I investigated the
more I saw he was right – 'he' being Jeremy Wright, who is now
a Conservative MP and Attorney General!

So although becoming a Christian had reinforced my Conservative beliefs, it is important to remember that this was an era
when the question was often posed, 'How can you be a Christian and a Conservative?' The landslide General Election defeat
in 1997 had left the party portrayed as rather selfish, corrupt
and only concerned with the economy, defence and Europe.
The importance of a peer group at this point in my journey
should not be underestimated, and under the leadership of Tim
Montgomerie the Conservative Christian Fellowship was a vital
part of the party's renewal. The CCF led the party to a renewed
focus on poverty, international development, the environment,
education, the family and One Nation Conservatism. I also met
various Christians I respected for their faith who were Conservatives: Gary Streeter MP, Philippa Stroud (now a special
advisor to Iain Duncan Smith) and Fiona Bruce, now MP for
Congleton.

So in 1998 I took the leap and joined the Tories – which
was still not very good for your Christian 'street cred'. But over
the years I have not doubted that decision and do not accept
that the main parties are just the same. Those on the centre-left
really do want the state to play such a central role that personal
responsibility as well as civic society gets squeezed out. This different foundation leads my party to promote localism and trust-
ing professionals such as head teachers to do their jobs. And I
personally hate the notion that the poor are the responsibility

only of the state; they are my responsibility, as I am commanded to love my neighbour. Such a biblical mandate extends way beyond paying my taxes to support the welfare system – which, of course, I also support.

However strident our political disagreements, in the UK we have the luxury of agreeing on the ends that politics should achieve, such as dealing with poverty, while disagreeing on the means to get there. This explains why Christians can be members of all the main political parties and why I believe our faith is best displayed by the trusted relationships built across the political spectrum. Some of my best friends in politics are members of the Labour Party . . .

Why I am a Green

Matt Valler

Matt Valler is a Green Party member and project director for the
Alchemy Project, an experimental community of practice committed to
reshaping young people's experience of the Bible. He has an MA from
London School of Theology and previously worked for Tearfund as National
Youthwork Coordinator and Project Leader.

Near the corner of my street there is a fire-pit that often burns
from a dilapidated front yard. It belongs to a mid-terrace pre-
fab from the 1950s; council house stock that was put up to last
ten years, but has not failed yet. Outside by the road there is
always some broken-down car, or van – the latest mechanical
project for the jobless tenants within. They are multi-generation
benefit claimants, well and truly locked into a cycle of welfare
dependency.

I live in a community of council tenants and owner-
occupiers. Recently several of our neighbours have had new,
taxpayer-funded kitchens fitted, something that as a working
family we can't afford. A few sit outside and drink all day, dis-
orderly adverts for welfare reform. But I do not begrudge them
my taxes, or their kitchens. Contrary to the prevailing media
mantra I don't regard them as skivers any more than I refer
to myself as a striver. The truth is, we are all profoundly disenfranchised. They are perhaps just a bit more so.

The skiver/striver myth is one created by a Conservative
press to divide and rule. While middle-income earners are busy
berating low-income welfare claimants, high-income bankers

and industry magnates avoid and evade taxes worth six times the annual budget for unemployment benefits.[1] The problem is not 'the economy, stupid'; it is much more serious than that. The problem is right at the heart of what makes us Britain. The problem is with our democracy.

We're so comfortable with our democracy that we take it for granted. Rogue states and wild dictators need democracy, of course. Surely we have it already! But democracy is more than just 'one person, one vote'. Real democracy is about truly having a voice. It's about being able to actively participate in and shape the society in which we live. Yet this kind of democracy is eroded every day in small ways as we drift further apart. Little by little, year by year, an unchecked capitalism has forced its way into our schools, hospitals, living rooms and bedrooms. We are now slaves to the markets, and we will even sacrifice our children to its gods.

This is not hyperbole. Since the coalition came to power in 2010, malnutrition cases in Britain have doubled as the government cut benefit payments while food prices rose dramatically.[2] Yet the same government refuses to raise corporation tax, claiming that large multinationals will remove themselves from London if they do. It is not democracy when the poor suffer while the rich are untouchable. It is not democracy when the richest 10 per cent of Londoners are 273 times better off than the poorest 10 per cent.[3] Because in a system that lives for economic growth, money equals power.

Green politics is about using the strength of the state to protect the rights of its citizens. We are no longer in the twentieth century. It is not state-heavy Communism that threatens us now; it is state-less Capitalism. An unregulated free market has led to rampant greenhouse-gas emissions, wages that no longer pay, and unaccountable multinationals whose whims dictate our economic policy. If we are to build a fair world we need to work together for genuine democratic participation. And that means growing an economy that works for everyone, not just the rich.

As a Christian I read the story of Jesus' death and resurrection as profoundly political. The crucifixion is a tool of political repression, but Jesus walks again in Galilee in defiance of Caesar's claim on his life. Democracy lives on the idea that even the weakest, most disenfranchised person can be included and given power to affect the destiny of our community. For me that is a sacred belief that arises from the empty tomb.

The Greens are the only party in British politics to make genuine democratic participation the cornerstone of their policy. From that core value arises a different vision of 'the state'. Instead of the great 'other', a behemoth that swallows our taxes and roars against our freedoms, a Green view of the state is based on community. We all own the state, we must all have equal power to influence it, and then together we can share in both its responsibilities and opportunities.

After the 2010 election I wrote to my newly elected Conservative MP asking him to protect the poorest in our constituency. He replied by saying that people on benefits need 'tough love'. I disagree. It is those with unchecked wealth who need tough love. The rest of us need freedom – the chance to shape our world together.

Why I am Labour

Stephen Timms

Stephen Timms has been MP for East Ham since 1994 and was re-elected in 2010 with the largest majority in the House of Commons. He is currently the Shadow Minister of State for Employment. Stephen is also the Labour Party Faith Envoy and Chair of Christians on the Left.

One summer holiday when I was a student, I helped out on a church mission at a gospel hall in Forest Gate, east London. I met people committed to serving Christ in the heart of a low-income community. It was only two weeks, but I was hooked. For the first time I saw how what I believed could shape the course of my life. When I found a job in London, I moved to the area. I joined the new church which the mission team had set up. And, wanting to become involved in the local community, I joined the Labour Party. I became the party secretary, a councillor and leader of the council. Twenty years ago I became the local MP.

Why Labour? The best summary I know of the basis for Christians to be involved in politics was given by Tom Wright, the former bishop of Durham: 'People who believe in the resurrection, in God making a whole new world in which everything will be set right at last, are unstoppably motivated to work for that new world in the present.' I would argue that Labour is the political movement today within which that work can best be undertaken.

Labour's heritage is steeped in faith. The party has deep roots in Christian socialism. Its early leaders, owing 'more to

Methodism than to Marx', put their livelihoods on the line for justice. They united great multitudes to stand up to the elite in defence of the ordinary. Many had the 'unstoppable motivation' fuelled by belief in the resurrection that Wright describes. Labour was founded on the affirmation of community, believing firmly that we can achieve more together than on our own. Nurturing common life, in a way very familiar to members of church congregations, makes Labour distinct from other political traditions.

We established the National Health Service in 1948. Decommodifying access to healthcare released working people from the grip of fear that ill health could drive them to penury. We should never forget what Bevan overcame and why he fought so tenaciously. More recently we introduced the minimum wage, put the Child Poverty Act on the statute book, invested in new school and hospital buildings and committed to the target set by the United Nations that 0.7 per cent of our GDP should be paid out in overseas aid. The final years of the last government were overtaken by the global financial crisis, but its achievements endure.

Work has an intrinsic dignity that is to be cherished. We are determined to end long-term youth unemployment with the Compulsory Jobs Guarantee. We want to tackle exploitative zero-hours contracts, which undermine family life. Labour market exploitation and human flourishing are incompatible. Too many companies, instead of acting responsibly, have cut the pay of those at the bottom and increased charges to their customers in order to finance enormous salaries for a few right at the top.

Many in the churches had high hopes when the coalition was elected. The Conservative Party seemed to represent traditional values. David Cameron spoke of 'the big society' and of harnessing the contribution of volunteers and faith groups. Iain Duncan Smith announced that job centres would be permitted to refer hard-up jobseekers to church-based food banks.

But demand at the food banks skyrocketed, as more and more people found themselves unable to afford enough food for their families. Deeply unfair measures like the bedroom tax – which Labour has pledged to scrap – have pushed large numbers who were just about keeping their finances above water into rent arrears and debt. Food bank volunteers have been shocked by the petty benefit rules and seemingly arbitrary 'sanctions' which have driven people to seek help. Three-quarters of a million people were helped by Trussell Trust food banks last year.

Arising from the work of its food banks, now numbering over 400, and the ideas of their church-based volunteers, the Trussell Trust has ideas for improving the benefit system without additional cost. Mr Duncan Smith refuses to meet them, accusing them of a 'political agenda'. Their crime? They refuse to keep quiet about rapidly growing numbers turning to them for help. Now, job centres are no longer allowed to refer jobseekers officially to them, but merely to 'signpost' them.

Hope in the Liberal Democrats evaporated when policies that had been presented as matters of principle before the election were quickly abandoned soon afterwards.

The Labour Party, with its commitment to stand up for the poorest, is a natural home for the 'unstoppable motivation' of people who believe in the resurrection. As followers of Christ we have a mandate to be involved, not to stand aloof in a holy huddle. I hope Christians around the country will accept the challenge and join us in the Labour Party. And support us at this next election to form a 'One Nation' government, bringing people together for the common good.

Why I am a Liberal Democrat

Steve Webb

Appointed Member of the Privy Council in July 2014, Steve Webb is also MP for Thornbury & Yate and the Minister of State for Pensions. He was previously MP for Northavon, where he was elected in 1997, 2001 and 2005, before the constituency was split into two new constituencies, including Thornbury & Yate.

There are good Christian people in all political parties, and any form of engagement by Christians in the political process is to be welcomed. But as a Liberal Democrat I find that my Christian values and beliefs fit particularly well with the founding values and approach of my party. I hope I can explain why in this short article.

The foreword to the constitution of the Liberal Democrats says that we seek to build a society in which 'no one shall be enslaved by poverty, ignorance or conformity'. It goes on to say that we 'champion the freedom, dignity and well-being of individuals, we acknowledge and respect their right to freedom of conscience and their right to develop their talents to the full'. As a list of values and priorities, this seems to me to be a list to which most Christians should be able to say 'Amen'!

To look at these in a bit more detail, a concern for social justice is an important part of the Liberal Democrat tradition. As a party that believes in freedom, there can be few things more enslaving to people than grinding poverty and debt. While we do not believe that money is the answer to people's problems, too many people are prevented from achieving their full potential because of poverty.

Worse still, these disadvantages can easily be passed on from generation to generation. That is why the Liberal Democrats are so committed to the idea of 'social mobility' and have championed in government things like the 'pupil premium', which diverts additional funding to the most disadvantaged children in order to help close the attainment gap which emerges so early in life.

The party's support for freedom of conscience and opposition to 'conformity' is also something that I know Christians will welcome. One of the fundamental human rights that we hold dear is freedom of religion, and we also believe that people shouldn't be forced to fit a mould. I firmly believe that we worship a God who rejoices in diversity and whose plan is about enabling us to be more fully ourselves rather than to turn us into something we are not. If God's plan is built on treating us as his children, rather than coercing us as slaves, then governments should surely be very wary of using the coercive power of the state to make people live their lives in a particular way.

This argument is expanded in more detail in the foreword that I wrote to a book published in 2012 by the Lib Dem Christian Forum, entitled *Liberal Democrats do God*. This collection of essays by Christian MPs and members of the House of Lords reflects the diversity of Christian expression within our party, but also shows the different ways in which their Christian faith influences the political outlook of the contributors.

There are many features of the Liberal Democrat identity that should come naturally to Christians. One of these is the internationalist, outward-looking nature of the party. We recognize that tackling the world's big problems, such as global terrorism, poverty, migration or climate change, requires countries to work together. While we recognize that international institutions such as the EU and the UN are imperfect, we firmly believe that narrow nationalism and isolationism serve neither our national interest nor the best interests of our common humanity. We also believe that insularity can quickly turn into hostility towards people who come to the UK seeking asylum or as economic migrants, and we condemn any attempts to demonize or dehumanize such people.

Liberal Democrats also firmly believe that we are stewards of the planet and that we need to pass it on to our children in a better state than we inherited it from our parents. We were the first major political party to talk seriously about the importance of environmental sustainability and tackling climate change, and in parliament we have regularly campaigned for things like a tougher Climate Change Act and more investment in renewable and low-carbon energy generation. For me as a Christian, taking good care of our planet for the benefit of future generations seems a pretty essential part of the political agenda of any party that I would want to be part of.

No one political party is a perfect fit for a Christian, and part of the point of political engagement is to enable people to shape the political party of which they are a member. But over more than two decades as a member of the Liberal Democrats I can say with conviction that our party is one whose instincts are repeatedly in tune with the values that many Christians hold dear.

Why I am UKIP

Robert Brown

Robert Brown is UKIP councillor for Ramsey, the first town council to be controlled by UKIP, taking nine out of 17 seats in the 2011 local elections. Robert joined UKIP in 2004 and was UKIP's parliamentary candidate for North West Cambridgeshire in 2005 and 2010, winning more votes in that election than any other UKIP candidate except Nigel Farage.

I believe UKIP's common-sense approach is the closest to being in line with God's word in serving the people. I appreciate that no political party is totally in line with the Bible, but UKIP is close to the top end and fares well on many things in line with Scripture. Starting with the name, UKIP:

- **United** – 1 Corinthians 1.10, 'Be of the same mind.' We all want the freedom to choose and not be dictated to by the EU.
- **Kingdom** – Matthew 12.25–37, 'How then will his kingdom stand?' By working together and obeying the laws it has agreed to follow from its leader.
- **Independence** – Acts 22.27–28, 'But I was born a citizen.' We are British-born citizens and we believe in a democracy that gives the right to choose.
- **Party** – 1 Corinthians 9.18–19, 'I have made myself a servant to all.' Politicians are elected to serve, not to lord it over the people they represent.

People in North West Cambridgeshire and Ramsey know that UKIP can be trusted to deliver on the local issues that are most important to them in their local communities. They also feel that UKIP can be trusted to deliver nationwide to solve the problems our country faces.

UKIP is the only party that is telling the people the truth about the EU. Only UKIP will make sure that we control our own borders, deciding who can come to live in this country and why. Only UKIP will create more grammar schools, so that people from all backgrounds can have access to every opportunity. Only UKIP is saying that we in the UK should decide what should happen to terrorists and criminals, rather than leaving such decisions to the increasingly irresponsible whims of the European court.

Above all, only UKIP will return the government of Britain back to Britain at Westminster. The European Union already has more control over how we are allowed to conduct our lives than our own elected government, but the EU still seeks to increase its powers over our country.

I know what needs to be done: we need to roll up our sleeves and lead by example in our communities and throughout the nation. For the first time, we have a serious opportunity to make it happen. Where other political parties are seeing their membership fall, more and more people are joining UKIP. We're consistently polling well ahead of the Lib Dems, making us the third force in British politics – and they're in government. We're winning votes all over the country, in parts of the south where Labour is nowhere and in parts of the north where the Conservatives have vanished.

More importantly, we're already changing the debate. Our ideas are forcing the other parties to accept policies they never would have backed otherwise. There's now genuine discussion around how many more people this country can afford to let in without our overstrained services and infrastructure falling apart. Following pressure from us, the Conservatives have even pledged a referendum on the European Union.

What we have done together here in Ramsey has already made a difference and what we've done as a party has already changed this country for the better.

The other political parties have made terrible mistakes and don't care about the people they are supposed to serve and represent. Our national debt is enormous, standing at £1.3 trillion. The fundamental values on which this country was built are being thrown away. Democracy itself has been turned upside down, with European bureaucrats who have never won a single vote telling our own elected politicians what to do.

Only UKIP is challenging the political consensus on these desperately important issues. That's why, despite all the media hostility, despite the huge imbalance of resources, despite the fact that we are pilloried or pushed out of the TV studio altogether when the BBC debates the big political questions, UKIP gains more supporters and members every day.

Most of our members come from ordinary working backgrounds and don't have millions of pounds from union funds. I've fought two General Elections on state benefits, doubling my vote each time. We don't have big business backing. Unlike other parties, we just have people who feel very passionate about our country because we know that our country deserves a lot better and we should govern our own nation for the benefit of its people.

We have found that we are not alone. There are already tens of thousands of paid-up members and that number is growing by the day. We have the ability to transform the country and to put the 'Great' back into Great Britain.

As a political party we should be taken seriously and be included in the big political debates that take place, as they affect us all. To us it doesn't matter if our policies are being adopted by the other political parties – we just want to see these common-sense policies put into practice.

At the General Election, if we win more seats than the Lib Dems we could hold the balance of power in the next coalition government. It's a real possibility and a goal to aim for in 2015. In order to achieve this, we have to level the playing field. Our message is becoming more and more powerful and we will make it work even with limited funds by hard work and commitment. We have a whole range of policies that we plan to keep quiet until just before the General Election campaign, and the best kind of people with a vast range of skills and talents to implement them, given half the chance.

In the past, people fought and died giving their lives to ensure that Britain stayed free and independent. We believe that every new member who joins UKIP will help restore common sense and good judgement on how best to build a better, brighter, freer and richer future for the country we all love.

That's the reason I joined the *only* party that believes in serving its people, who want to be led and governed by honest politicians from Westminster − and nowhere else.

Conclusion

We live in the age of the hashtag and the text message. We are used to fast food, on-demand TV and one-click ordering. If something we want takes too long or too much effort to obtain, there are plenty of other options available.

The problem is that this diffusion of consumerism has stretched far beyond what we buy and watch on our TVs and computer screens. It has permeated every area of our lives, including the news and the way we engage with our politicians – and, just as importantly, the way they engage with us. Our culture is one of instant gratification and soundbites. The days of the grand vision are gone. Politics is fast becoming another consumer product: one that has to work for us if it is to hold our attention. If one party doesn't give us everything we want, we move to another – or, more likely, opt out altogether.

The reality is that politics does not and cannot work like this, and neither does our faith. Politics is not like a TV we can turn off because it doesn't happen to be showing anything we want to watch. Although Prime Minister's Question Time does bear passing similarities to a pantomime or reality TV show, we can't boo people off the stage or vote them out of the House. Behind the jeering and the shouts of 'Order!' are real issues that impact all of us, and that most politicians work extremely hard to understand and address in the interests of the electorate.

A common complaint of politicians is, 'They're all the same. Nothing ever changes.' At election time, this sentiment feeds voter apathy and allows incumbent politicians to remain in office. But we are also quite wrong to expect our politicians to fix every problem facing us. We cannot expect real change to come about simply through ticking one or other box on a ballot sheet, and then sitting back for the next five years and letting 650 MPs make all the decisions that affect the lives of the 60 million people they represent. Similarly, expressing our faith must be something that is worked out in our daily lives, not left to the pastors and paid 'professional' Christians, or confined to occasional gestures. In both cases we need to get our hands dirty. That will inevitably require sacrifice and risk.

Jesus said, 'The poor you will always have with you, and you can help them any time you want.' Politicians and political parties come and go, but some things remain the same. Regardless of who is in government, there will always be injustice. Reform will always be needed. Bringing this about is not just the work of elected officials: it is the work of the kingdom.

James 4.17 reads: 'Anyone, then, who knows the good they ought to do and doesn't do it, sins.' As Christians we all have a commission to bring about change in society. The political system has its faults, and we should work to address these, but an *over*emphasis on the shortcomings of our politicians provides a pretext to sidestep the personal nature of this call and gives us an excuse not to engage directly with the issues that matter the most. Moreover, the commission is not a five-yearly one: it is for now, and for the rest of our lives. Voting should be the *reflection* of our ongoing activity to bring about God's kingdom – not the limit of that activity.

Notes

1 Engaging with politics

1 Nick Spencer, *Votewise* (London: SPCK, 2004), p. 11.

2 Andrew Rawnsley, *Servants of the People* (London: Penguin, 2001), p. 13.

3 See <www.ukpolitical.info/Turnout45.htm> and.

4 <www.telegraph.co.uk/news/uknews/1429109/Campbell-interrupted-
Blair-as-he-spoke-of-his-faith-We-dont-do-God.html>.

5 Nick Spencer, *The Bible and Politics: Christian Sources of British Political
Thought* (Cambridge: Jubilee Centre, 2012).

6 See <www.respublica.org.uk/item/Benedict-Red-Tories-and-Blue-
Labour>.

7 In fact, the practice of turning to face the wall is said to result from the
difficulty members of each House would have in kneeling to pray when
wearing a sword.

8 This section of the chapter was written with extensive help from Andy
Flannagan, Director of Christians on the Left.

9 See further the section on the environment in Chapter 3.

10 <www.christianitymagazine.co.uk/Browse-By-Category/features/Can-
Christians-save-politics.aspx>.

11 <www.comres.co.uk/polls/Premier_Gay_Marriage_data_tables_Nov11.
pdf>.

12 For a detailed overview of marriage and divorce in the Bible, see
Jonathan Burnside, *God, Justice and Society* (Oxford: Oxford University
Press, 2011), pp. 317–45, also pp. 347–87.

13 See, for example, Jonathan Burnside's assessment of 2 Samuel 13 in *God,
Justice and Society*, pp. 327–9.

14 For more on this idea and the way the Bible provides a coherent
framework, see Guy Brandon, *The Jubilee Roadmap* (Cambridge: Jubilee
Centre, 2012).

15 Brandon, *Jubilee Roadmap*, p. 4.

16 Samantha Callan, Centre for Social Justice. See <www.bbc.co.uk/news/
uk-politics-24309634>.

17 <www.centreforsocialjustice.org.uk/policy/pathways-to-poverty>.

18 In *Lies (and the Lying Liars Who Tell Them)* (London: Penguin, 2003).
19 <www.bbc.co.uk/news/uk-23265810>.
20 See <www.christiantoday.com/article/christians.divided.over.same.sex.
marriage/32159.htm>.
21 See <www.comres.co.uk/polls/C4M_European_Voting_Intention_
Poll_15_May_2014.pdf>.
22 For example, <http://blogs.spectator.co.uk/coffeehouse/2013/05/
same-sex-marriage-bill-how-mps-voted/>.

2 UK plc

1 See <www.ipsos-mori.com/researchspecialisms/socialresearch/
specareas/politics/trends.aspx>.
2 Robert F. Kennedy, address to the University of Kansas, March 1968.
3 See Richard Layard, *Happiness: Has Social Science A Clue?*, Lionel
Robbins Memorial Lectures 2002/03, No. 1. See online at <http://cep.
lse.ac.uk/events/lectures/layard/RL030303.pdf>.
4 Will Hutton, in *The Observer*, 1999.
5 Figures from Credit Action; see <www.creditaction.org.uk/helpful-
resources/debt-statistics.html>.
6 For more on the differences between different types of immigrant in
Israelite society, see the section on immigration in Chapter 3.
7 <www.theguardian.com/politics/2013/jan/08strivers-shirkers-
language-welfare>.
8 <www.theguardian.com/commentisfree/2012/feb/02/workless-
families-convenient-truth-editorial>.
9 In the coming years six means-tested benefits will be replaced by the
Universal Credit system.
10 <http://news.bbc.co.uk/1/hi/uk_politics/298745.stm>.
11 <www.bbc.co.uk/news/uk-politics-15996253>.
12 <www.publications.parliament.uk/pa/cm199900/cmselect/
cmscotaf/59/5908.htm>.
13 <www.bbc.co.uk/news/uk-politics-25225532>.
14 <www.fabians.org.uk/wp-content/uploads/2012/12/Beveridge-
supplement_WEB_SPREADS.pdf>.

3 The global perspective

1 Excluding Croatia, which is expected to join in the future.
2 See UKIP report at <www.brugesgroup.com/CostOfTheEU2008.pdf>.
3 See <www.thisismoney.co.uk/money/news/article-2268846/Should-
Britain-stay-European-Union.html>.
4 See <http://en.wikipedia.org/wiki/Proposed_referendum_on_United_
Kingdom_membership_of_the_European_Union#Opinion_polling>.

5   <www.bbc.co.uk/news/business-24859486>.
6   <www.bbc.co.uk/news/uk-politics-22396690>.
7   See Nick Spencer, *Apolitical Animal* (Cambridge: Jubilee Centre, 2003), chapter 3.
8   Paul Mills and Michael Schluter, *Should Christians Support the Euro?* (Cambridge: Jubilee Centre, 1998).
9   See the CBI's report, pp. 7–11, <www.cbi.org.uk/global-future/>.
10 Estonia, Latvia, Lithuania, Poland, Czech Republic, Slovakia, Hungary and Slovenia.
11 <www.bbc.co.uk/news/uk-27407126>.
12 If the *nokrî* was not charged interest, he could borrow freely from the Israelites and make money by lending at interest elsewhere. Leviticus 25.35–37 shows that the *ger* was to be treated the same as the native Israelite.
13 See further the section on the economy in Chapter 2.
14 'David Cameron: this is the greenest government ever', *The Guardian*, 26 April 2012. See <www.theguardian.com/environment/2012/apr/26/david-cameron-greenest-government-ever>.
15 See 'Failure to stop Chancellor from undermining efforts to cut carbon pollution and support for fracking means Lib Dems are no longer green, say charities', *The Independent*, 13 September 2013, <www.independent.co.uk/news/uk/politics/failure-to-stop-chancellor-from-undermining-efforts-to-cut-carbon-pollution-and-support-for-fracking-means-lib-dems-are-no-longer-green-say-charities-8812921.html>.
16 He later made a controversial apology for this comment.
17 Hilary Marlow, 'The Environment', in R. Lynas (ed.), *Votewise Now!* (London: SPCK, 2009), p. 50.

4 Public services

1   <www.visionofhumanity.org/pdf/ukpi/UK_Peace_Index_report_2013.pdf>.
2   <www.bbc.co.uk/news/uk-25858421>.
3   <www.conservatives.com/News/News_stories/2011/10/Tough_on_crime_and_tough_on_criminals.aspx>.
4   F. Brown, S. Driver and C. Briggs, *Hebrew and English Lexicon* (BDB) (Peabody, MA: Hendrickson, 1997). Unless stated otherwise all Hebrew definitions are taken from this lexicon.
5   Tim Keller, *Generous Justice* (London: Hodder & Stoughton, 2010); cf. <www.relevantmagazine.com/god/practical-faith/what-biblical-justice>.
6   Jonathan Burnside, *God, Justice and Society* (Oxford: Oxford University Press, 2011), p. 27.

7   See 'Ethics', *Dictionary of the Old Testament I: Pentateuch* (Downers Grove, IL: InterVarsity Press, 2003), pp. 224–9.

8   Jonathan Burnside, 'Criminal Justice', in R. Lynas (ed.), *Votewise Now!* (London: SPCK, 2009), p. 26.

9   <www.publications.parliament.uk/pa/cm201213/cmselectcmhaff/184/18409.htm>.

10 <www.theguardian.com/politics/2001/may/23/labour.tonyblair>.

11 <www.reform.co.uk/content/4147/imported_content/epublications/the_week/michael_gove_why_the_sums_dont_add_up_when_it_comes_to_raising_school_standards>.

12 Guy Brandon, *Education in the Bible: A Starting Point for Discussion* (Cambridge: Jubilee Centre, 2013).

13 <www.rabbisacks.org/covenant-conversation-5771-haazinu-the-inheritance-that-belongs-to-everyone/>.

14 <http://relationalschools.org/responding-to-ofsted-the-purpose-of-schooling/>.

15 Nigel Lawson, *The View from No. 11: Memoirs of a Tory Radical* (London: Bantam Press, 1992).

16 <www.bmj.com/content/343/bmj.d4817>.

17 <www.publications.parliament.uk/pa/cm201213/cmhansrd/cm121127/debtext/121127-0001.htm>.

18 Ian McColl, 'National Priorities for Health', in A. Vale (ed.), *Our National Life* (Oxford: Monarch Books, 1998). See Nick Spencer, *Votewise* (London: SPCK, 2004), p. 72.

19 <www.bbc.co.uk/news/health-21667065>.

5 The relational manifesto

1   This chapter was written with the help of Michael Schluter.

2   'Report Details How Lehman Hid Its Woes', *New York Times*, 11 March 2010.

3   See further the section on the economy in Chapter 2.

4   Paul Mills and Michael Schluter, *After Capitalism: Rethinking Economic Relationships* (Cambridge: ECPF and Jubilee Centre, 2012), p. 111.

5   See John Ashcroft and David Wong, *Progressive Families, Progressive Britain: Why Britain Needs Family Proofing of Policy* (Cambridge: Relationships Foundation, 2010).

6   This idea was pioneered by the Relationships Foundation, <www.relationshipsfoundation.org>.

6 Why vote for . . . ?

1   <www.taxresearch.org.uk/Blog/2013/09/13/benefit-errors-cost-1-million-a-day-tax-avoidance-and-evasion-cost-260-million-a-day/>,